YOUR MIND
KNOWS MORE
THAN YOU DO

YOUR MIND KNOWS MORE THAN YOU DO

THE SUBCONSCIOUS SECRETS OF SUCCESS

Blue Dolphin Publishing

Sidney
FRIEDMAN

Published by
Blue Dolphin Publishing, Inc.
P.O. Box 8, Nevada City, CA 95959
Web site: http://www.bluedolphinpublishing.com
Orders: 1-800-643-0765

ISBN: 1-57733-052-8

Library of Congress Cataloging-in-Publication Data

Friedman, Sidney L.
    Your mind knows more than you do : the sub-
conscious secrets of success / Sidney Friedman.
        p.   cm.
    Includes bibliographical references.
    ISBN 1-57733-052-8
    1. Success—Psychological aspects.   2. Subcon-
sciousness.   I. Title.
BF637.S8F667 1999
168'.1—dc21   98-55506
                                                  CIP

Cover art: Tim Turbett
Jacket layout: Lito Castro
Inside photos: Larry Dermody
Photo of author: Tom Cruze (used by permission of the
    Chicago Sun-Times)
Retouching: John Bresnahan

Printed in the United States of America

10   9   8   7   6   5   4   3

Table of Contents

I

The
Hidden
Mind

I

The Hidden Mind

"I couldn't wait for success. So I went ahead without it."
— Jonathan Winters

Hidden help. The invisible. Some people doubt what can't be seen. Others believe in magical things. This book is for both. If you are one of the former, suspend your current assumptions and apprehensions for just a while, stay with the enclosed concepts for even a few weeks, give them a chance. Explicitly follow the exercises. Something remarkable may happen.

Is there a way to overcome difficulties and achieve great success in business, friendship, love and family? There exists a power which is the avenue toward achievement and gratification. You may use it if you desire. It is not necessarily mystical or mysterious, except that it is not known by the majority of people. Throughout the ages a charmed few have understood this knowledge. Be it part of their nature or be it something they acquired, with this force they have made their wishes materialize.

You will learn an approach using time-tested techniques and exercises that will allow your conscious mind to make use of the knowledge contained in vast areas of the brain usually unavailable to us. You will learn the subconscious language of success, a method of communication that will allow you to literally ask your subconscious questions, and then receive reliable, clear answers from it.

Success is a result of finding solutions and taking actions. With diligence, you will learn to use your ENTIRE mind to help make difficult decisions and creatively solve problems by effectively consulting your true innate desires and wisdom. You will learn to focus your subconscious to compel you to fully act upon the solutions.

More simply, you will learn to transfer subconscious information to your conscious mind, then you will learn to transfer your conscious thoughts and desires to your subconscious mind.

Over the years, students of these techniques have discovered their real feelings about personal and business relationships, they have uncovered hidden talents and interests, they have increased their capacity for creativity, they have made strong career choices, they have become more organized and productive, they have made many wishes come true, and they have developed a strong and healthy belief in themselves.

At one of the most spiritual and magical places on earth, a seat of Western civilization, the temple of Apollo at Delphi, a Greek philosopher inscribed two simple words: "Know thyself." This modest, unadorned phrase is the starting point for attaining aspirations. It represents a seemingly easy task but in reality is the most difficult thing to accomplish. How do you truly do it? How do you really know what lies within? If you actually "know thyself," an essential step has been taken toward the goal of a successful, satisfied life. The thoughts and tools within these pages will help in this exploration. In addition, any intuitive powers you already possess

will become amplified, more effective and pro-
nounced, with results bordering on the incredible.

**Read the contents slowly, deliberately,
repeatedly,** and be warned that speed reading is for-
bidden. Either do the exercises as you read them, or
better yet, read through the book, then go back and
execute the exercises while reading the book a second
time. Continue to use these tools regularly. Make a
commitment. Many people read an enlightening book
or attend a motivating seminar which inflates them
with confidence and direction, only to have the impact and glow wear off after a few days. Again, I stress
the importance of reading and rereading this material.
And again, I emphasize the value of doing the exercises no matter how unusual they may seem to you at
first. Their effectiveness will soon become apparent.

Keep in mind a primary principle of the concepts to follow: In just about everything, there is a
perpetual swing back and forth. There is a motion
created from desire and emotion, a rise and fall, a
pressure and release, a daybreak and nightfall, a
coming and going, an expansion and contraction, a
powerful pendulum inherent in practically everything
throughout our world and beyond.

Become aware of the sway, feel the flux, connect with the movement, and you will live with success.

When this happens, the shifts in nature, business and relationships become apparent. Truths become evident. Secrets are revealed. Moments matter. The time between beginnings and endings expands. Magic happens.

II

Journey

II

Journey

For a number of years I have made my living demonstrating extended mental abilities and the art of magical thinking to corporations, organizations and individuals. Engineers, doctors, computer programmers, sales people, executives, factory workers, housewives, househusbands, teachers, artists, people from all walks of life and from a variety of professions have witnessed these presentations. Some of the feats are natural abilities, some of them I have discovered and developed, and all of them I have had to work on repetitively day after day, year after year, until I reached a reliable proficiency and accuracy. These are skills which most people hear about but never have the chance to view in person. Those who see these presentations, continually urge me to share this valuable information with a wider audience, thus these pages are written.

To become more perceptive, to intuit private thoughts and feelings, to listen to your hunches, to intuitively anticipate the future, even to influence the future, to imagine, to create, and to use the mind in ways that can make wishes and dreams come to fruition are all possible for you.

We are in an era where the machines often humble the minds. The paradox is that the minds invented the machines, so don't be humbled for a second. And, as you will see, we are entering an era where the mind and spirit will evolve new, unprecedented abilities and powers.

As a child, as long as I can remember, I have been fascinated with magical things, any achievement which defies the existing limits. It extended from finding lost objects, like my mother's ring or a friend's baseball, just by picturing them in my mind.

At the age of eight or nine I began seeking more information. Given to me as gifts or borrowed from the library, some of the books I read contained the sleight-of-hand "trick" kind of magic. I became acquainted with some of these stunts which were entertaining but did not fulfill the search.

A few other sources wrote about witchcraft, spells and occult topics—most of which seemed possibly destructive, discomforting and, as I have discovered over time, are filled with inconsistencies, contradictions and an air of negativity. Then and now, I like things that are comforting, peaceful and positive.

The true magic I found was in the stories about, and the deeds of, the Milton Hersheys, the Conrad Hiltons, the Kathryn Hepburns, the Jackie Robinsons, people who thought independently, achieved great things and had some enchantment in their lives. A list of these people throughout history, whether well-known or private, could fill many pages of this book, but the point is that in combination with their unimpeded desire for success, there was a force, a power, a science, some sort of factor, whether they were aware of it or not, that made their wishes come true.

It matters not from where a person comes. Whether he or she began in poverty or wealth, from acceptance or rejection, there are examples of achievement in a democratic, free society from both sides of these fences, even from under the fence. What matters, of course, is where and how one ends up. What matters is the destination and the journey. What matters is self-belief, feeling valuable, recognizing yourself as important. It is the beginning of magic and greatness.

Ironically, it seems the moment you decide not to impress anyone but yourself is the moment the road to greatness begins. It is the moment you begin to make some discernible difference in the world and for your family. It is the inauguration of genius. It is the start of an honest, creative, meaningful and magical life.

True independence begets enchantment, strength, beauty and art. True self-reliance brings tranquility to the heart. This confidence, when sustained, takes us to our dreams and the fulfillment of our wishes. It also engenders love, the kind of acceptance we seek most, yet usually fail to receive when we aim to please with hopes of reciprocation, indulgently intent on adoration, rather than purely giving without condition. But truth, confidence and a sense of self actually bring others close to us, because now they see and know who we really are.

Some people possess this self-aware quality naturally. Maybe it's in their genes or from a special upbringing. Some are acquainted with this trait, but rarely sustain the state. Most must climb to get there.

And when you're there, and work to stay there, what a sight it is. The view of the world and all its wonders is clear, defined and inviting. You can look back and realize that when there was little or no progress in your life, somewhere there was fear. Now, when there is no fear, there is progress. There is respect and reverence for unexplained powers, but the anxiety is gone. Life moves and develops. The journey is rich.

How do you get there? Parts of the map follow. Other parts you will forge on your own.

As concisely yet completely as possible, you will be exposed to three things: specific exercises and devices to make good things happen, ideas for vitality and growth, and metaphors and answers about our existence to add to or weigh against your own convictions.

All of these tools form a miraculous system which, when used properly, will help get you to your destination. It is about magical thinking and for the first time it is tangible. Above all, it is a method that links the subconscious to the conscious mind. The conscious mind knows a limited amount of information. The subconscious mind seems to know just about everything, and from here on, it will be your friend and teacher.

III

The
Pendulum
Principle

III

The Pendulum Principle

Building an Information Superhighway
Between the Conscious and Subconscious

To begin, we will learn the use of one of the most fascinating, yet easily mastered devices ever known.

Life seems to move to and fro. There is an ebb and flow to just about everything. There is a push and a pull, an inhalation and an exhalation, a tension and a release. It happens with the ocean and its tides, with the atmosphere and its pressure, with molecular reactions, with the universe, with all creation, with love-making, with birth, with digestion, with the stock market, with the building of muscle, and with the building of inner strength. The sweep back and forth of life can be viewed daily at every moment, and in a few moments it will be viewed in your very own hands.

Those who have mastered this device have achieved great sight into the future and insight into the present. Those who have worked with it and who have attained the knack of its use, have taken giant steps toward reaching their goals. And with this technique, those who have explored, respected and tapped the subconscious have found some answers they may not have found otherwise. What's more, if you believe that many causes of our actions and future actions lie in our subconscious, then a mechanism to communicate with the subconscious and anticipate these actions must be developed. With the information in this book, it is now available to us all.

A basic dictionary definition describes the CONSCIOUS as "that part of a person's mental activity of which he is fully aware at any given time." The SUBCONSCIOUS is defined as "occurring without the conscious perception or only with a slight perception on the part of the individual." In other words, conscious activities are things you have to think through, whereas subconscious actions are more instinctual, such as swallowing, blinking, breathing, and certain innate abilities.

For the device we are about to learn, here is a key:

The transfer of a positive action or thought from the conscious to the subconscious, or vice versa, is magical in the truest sense of the word, and leads us to a content, enchanted life.

Enchantment is eventual accomplishment without conscious effort. It is the natural realization of a desire. Following years of conscious work and thousands of swings, when the golfer no longer consciously thinks of his arms, hips, head, grip, stance, motion and speed, when all of the many elements of a golf swing become instinctive, when that transfer from the conscious to the subconscious is complete, success is inevitable. When first learning multiplication tables in grammar school, a student must consciously think through each equation to come up with the solution until after many days and weeks of practice and repetition, the subconscious takes over and the answer to nine times eight becomes "second nature." The same phenomenon happens with typing on a keyboard, driving an automobile, playing a musical instrument, and equally so, with effective communication, organized work habits, true loving, and creativity, regardless of any less than prime examples of these capacities one may have been imprinted with as a child. Those imprints are not eternal. Only fear prevents a human being from reinventing himself. With time, patience, repetition and determination, the ineffective can be drained from the subconscious and the productive can be poured in.

Again, when the transfer of an action and desire from the conscious to the subconscious is complete, success is inevitable. Likewise, when we become aware of knowledge and skill lying within our subconscious, when we discover our natural abilities, when our buried knowledge and feelings are brought to the fore, when that transfer occurs, expect the same enchanted results. Each being has natural aptitudes like the herding capability of the border collie, the mothering skill of a robin, or perhaps the hunches of a successful businessman. Awareness of these talents, sensing deep feelings and discovering lost knowledge, consciously tuning in to the sub-conscious, allows one to "know thyself," to know the soul, and to begin the journey to contentment.

The conscious mind contains a narrow amount of information in comparison to the sub-conscious mind which, in a manner of speaking,

seems to know just about everything of importance to us.

What if there were a way to tap the subconscious, to get "on line" with it and make its vast information more readily available? What if there were a way to help us become more sensitive to the instincts buried deep within? And what if we were to add these insights to all the wisdom of our conscious mind? In tandem they would make us quite powerful to grow, understand and achieve.

Poet e.e. cummings once stated, "The more we know, the less we feel." This isn't true in all instances for all people, but I know to what he was referring: In the post World War II era (and beyond) of exponentially increased knowledge and tremendous rationality, our sensitivities can be dulled. We tend to ignore our intuitive side. For many of us in a 21st-century, computerized era this seems to be a tendency, and for many of us it keeps us from success.

Realize that the most accomplished people seem to have a knack, be it God-given or acquired, to combine their rationality with their sensitivity. They don't rely solely on logic. They use their mind with their heart, their cognitive side with their intuitive side, the Apollonian with the Dionysian. The enlightened, like Beethoven, achieve balance between reason and passion, not unlike The Great Wallenda or Philippe Petit on their high-wires, steadily striding the fine line between the two.

How do we achieve this equilibrium and tranquility? How do we make the subconscious our friend and mentor? Here is a step-by-step program and the first device to help realize this power and all the abundance that comes with it. If you are willing to work on it, your resourcefulness, confidence and capabilities will unfold and flourish.

There are many ways of communicating with the subconscious, but after years of study and years of working with thousands of people, for those who wish for direct access, what follows is truly impressive and effective.

It sounded unusual when I first heard about this, but like me, you must try what I am about to describe. Begin by obtaining a piece of cotton sewing thread about 10 to 14 inches long. A straight hair or a thin flexible gold or silver chain of the same length also works well. With a knot or a clasp, attach one end onto a ring or a metal washer or even a key, as long as the object has some weight to it. A gold gentleman's wedding band is about the right weight. Something meaningful often works better. A piece of quartz or a glass crystal with a grommet to attach the thread are also effective. Take the free end of the thread (or chain) and hold it with your thumb and forefinger, allowing the weighted end to hang (see **Sample Photographs**).

This tool is called the pendulum.

Of the devices and methods designed to talk with the subconscious mind, this miraculous mechanism is perhaps the most direct and effective with which to start. There are advanced levels for its use, but in the beginning it requires only a short time to make it work with the possibility of answering many of the questions we have in everyday life.

In response to your questions, the pendulum will either swing back and forth in a line or it will rotate in a circle. If you've raised an eyebrow, bear with me on this. Keep an open mind.

Follow these guidelines step by step.

Find a softly lit, quiet area with as few distractions as possible. Seat yourself in a comfortable chair with your legs uncrossed, feet flat on the floor, and begin by holding the pendulum in what we will call **the rest position** with the weighted end dangling still and the free end held gently between the thumb and forefinger as if it were a delicate treasure. Hold it a foot or so in front of you (in your right hand if you are a righty, in your left if you are a lefty) with your body relaxed and breathing normally. Your elbow may be resting on a table or it may be free.

Think this thought first: "**YES.**" Think of the word "**YES.**" Think it deliberately in your mind over and over again, then once slowly out loud, then continually in your mind again, **and the pendulum will begin to swing back and forth in a straight line.**

It will move on its own.

It may move only a little at first but **IT WILL** genuinely swing back and forth in a straight line.

The straight line movement will be your "**YES**" response to questions. It will remain your "**YES**" response for the rest of your life.

When you are doing this, do not try to actually physically move the pendulum yourself. **It will begin to move on its own.** It may happen right away or it may take awhile, but believe it or not, the pendulum will go into motion as if it had a life of its own.

THIS IS IMPORTANT: When at first it moves only a tiny bit, don't stop it. Let it keep moving. And once it begins to move just a little, allow it to swing into a larger sweep back and forth. Keep it going back and forth. Picture the thought. In your mind, encourage it. Back and forth, back and forth.

If, for some reason, nothing happens, put it aside for a few minutes, do something else, then return to it, repeating the above instructions. Sixty-five percent of the people I've worked with find immediate response. About thirty percent must do the procedure a few times before it happens. The rest have results within a day or two.

When you can do this procedure consistently, allow it to swing for a little while. Keep thinking "**YES,**" then after a minute or so, clear your mind and actually **will** the pendulum to stop. Desire it. It will come to a rest.

When you can reliably clear your mind and stop the pendulum to **the rest position**, then think of "**NO**" and imagine the pendulum going around in a circle. If you have mastered "**YES**," this should come in a snap. The circular movement will always be the "**NO**" response to your questions.

Do this for a couple of days and the reaction time of the pendulum will be quick and robust. When this happens, you are ready for the next step.

In the next chapter you will discover how to feed your subconscious with a desire so the subconscious can help make it a reality, but your first exercises with the pendulum are designed to develop your confidence and abilities in using it.

Exercise #1:

Ask questions to which you already know the answers. This may seem ridiculous, but this exercise is extremely useful in the development of your abilities. The questions should be simple and direct: Is my hair brown? Am I twenty-seven years old? Is the sun shining today? Is my favorite color blue?

Find a quiet place, hold the pendulum properly in "the rest position," and ask it these or similar ques-

tions. Take time with each question. See how the pendulum responds. Continue this process over and over again. If the pendulum responds quickly, strongly and correctly time after time, then you are ready to continue on to yet another level. If not, put it aside and come back to it later. Practice the "YES-NO" exercises until you have corrected any communications problems.

It is important to learn to clear your mind of all other thoughts prior to stating the question, and then to keep it clear while waiting for the response. For a few people this is difficult and hinders them from getting past this first exercise, so here are some "focus" skills to assist you if needed:

A) Put the pendulum down. In a quiet room, sit comfortably but with good posture, arms at your side, feet flat on the floor and your legs uncrossed; then with a long, slow inhale and exhale, breathe twice.

B) Now close your eyelids and roll your eyeballs up at a very SLIGHT angle.

C) With your eyes in that position, take several more long, slow breaths.

D) Roll your eyeballs back down to their normal position, slowly open your eyes and pick up the pendulum with your right hand if you are a righty, with your left hand if you are a lefty.

E) **Think of the pendulum as an extension of your body.**
   Gently, hold it in the rest position and close your eyes
   again, rolling your eyeballs SLIGHTLY up.

F) Breathe normally and think of the question, keeping
   your eyelids closed for at least five full seconds.

G) Very slowly open your eyelids. Look down at the
   pendulum. It may be in motion already.

You will not have to go through this focussing
process every time, but as a beginner it may be crucial
in achieving good results, and as you become more
advanced it will be a dependable warm-up prior to the
more consequential questions.

●

We will now move into an area where the
pendulum will respond to questions to which we do
not consciously know the answers. As mentioned
before, while the conscious mind knows a limited
amount of information, the subconscious seems to
grasp and know just about everything. Over the years,
I have become more and more aware of this fact. A
friend of mine experiences this phenomenon in his
dreams. He is a leading advertising executive in Chicago. He takes a cerebral approach to everything and

as he put it to me, "I'm the last one to believe in anything that is not proven by science and with 15 controlled tests." Nevertheless, he now believes in the all-knowing power of the subconscious because he has had a number of amazingly intuitive dreams in his life.

For example, one morning he awoke remembering a vivid dream in which an associate in his firm came to him explaining she had a degenerative illness and might have to leave work for a while to get treatment. He couldn't stop thinking about the dream, especially since the woman seemed the picture of health and never confided in him about any physical problems. It was strange for him to even think such a thing, so when he arrived at work he called the woman into his office and had to tell her about it. Her face turned pale as she said, "Oh my God! I've been tossing this around in my mind for over a week, and I've been debating whether to tell you. Although physically it's not a problem now, I have been diagnosed with the early stage of Multiple Sclerosis." Then, of course, **his** face turned a bit paler.

Somehow, his subconscious picked up on her situation. Prior to that meeting, she never told any of her fellow workers and for the most part she did not have interaction with him in the office since most of his work did not involve her, but his intuitive side revealed its knowledge in his dream.

On another occasion, he dreamt his wife's first cousin had tears in her eyes telling him she really needed to talk to Susan, his wife. She said, "Please wake up Susan right now. I have to speak to her about something urgent and I need her advice." The two women do not have much of a relationship and rarely communicate, but he told Susan about the dream and said perhaps she should call her anyway since maybe there's something wrong. Susan waited a couple of weeks. When they finally talked, it turned out her cousin's husband had moved out of the house on the night of that dream.

Subsequently, with his developed belief in the all-knowing power of the subconscious, he has made numerous shrewd business decisions and has willed many magical successes in his life. Since I taught him the techniques in this book, his quiet belief has grown so much, he seems to have developed a skill for knowing what will happen before it actually happens. With the aid of the pendulum you may develop the same awareness of what your subconscious is telling you, what others are trying to tell you, and even an anticipation of the future.

This exercise is the next step along the path. You will need an older member of your family, someone who witnessed your childhood.

Exercise #2:

Get yourself comfortable, hold the pendulum in the rest position, then ask a question about yourself for which you don't consciously remember the answer, yet your family member can confirm. Most likely it should be something involved with your early childhood. "Were my first intelligible words 'Mama'?" "Were my first intelligible words 'Dada'?" "Did I begin to walk at 13 months?" "Did I begin to walk at 15 months?" A member of your family or a close family friend could probably verify the accuracy of the pendulum's response. Do this with at least a half-dozen questions.

Your accuracy should be somewhere between 70% and 90% before continuing on to the next exercise. If your accuracy rate is lower, go back to review the earlier steps before proceeding. Sloppiness in the beginning will hinder your progress later.

At this point it is important to mention that, as you will soon learn, the pendulum can help all of us with making a goal come to fruition, but additionally, each of us develops other areas of expertise with this instrument. Some of us are better at finding lost objects with it, some are more adept at recovering memories, some are proficient with it for decision making, some for understanding the thoughts and actions of others. For all, it makes us more sensitive to our instincts and helps us to act upon our hunches and true desires. It can help to confirm ideas when problem solving. The important thing for now is not to worry so much about total accuracy, as long as the greater majority of responses are correct.

Exercise #3:

Ask questions about someone else, questions to which you could not possibly know the answers. This person, if not present, should be available to you to verify the answers. Though I've had success doing it by phone, in the beginning, their presence seems to help with the outcome. Most important, it should be someone who has positive thoughts about what you are doing. At this point you do not need any negative forces to interfere with your progress. For example, ask him or her, "Do you like broc-

coli?", "Do you like tomatoes?", "Is your favorite color blue?", "Are you wearing boxer shorts?", "Are you wearing briefs?", "Was your first kiss at the age of thirteen?", "Was your first kiss at the age of sixteen?"

This exercise should be done with a number of different people. Do it continually for weeks: any time someone visits your home, at lunch hour with a coworker, at a party, with neighbors, with friends. And it does not take much time. Don't accost them with it, just work it into your conversation. When it's appropriate tell them you have something exciting you've been experimenting with and want to know if they can help you for a few moments. Most people are receptive, positive and intrigued about what you are doing and will be willing participants for five or ten minutes. In addition, you will be surprised how many of these people will now wish to explore the possibilities of the pendulum for themselves. If once in a while someone is negative, after a minute thank them for their help and, of course, change the subject.

Here is an exercise people love, but it may take some time, up to nine months, before you get confirmation of your answer.

Exercise #4:

Hold the pendulum two to three inches above the abdomen of a pregnant woman, especially if she is at least two months pregnant. If the pendulum swings back and forth in a straight line, the baby will be a boy. If it moves around in a circular pattern, paint the room pink. The accuracy of this test is uncanny and it works best with the woman's own wedding ring or her husband's. If they already know the sex, you have instant verification, but even if the couple has had an ultrasound, most people tell their doctors they want the baby's sex to be a surprise, so you will have to wait a few months, but the call you get will be very exciting.

A warning: Absolutely do not use your pendulum to answer questions about an unborn baby's health, or for that matter, anyone else's health. If someone asks you about a medical matter, the answers will most likely result in an affirmative response that everything will be all right. Why is this so? Our extreme emotions affect the pendulum's answer. Even if we do not know the people, most of us want a fellow human being to be healthy and well, so much so, we cannot stay emotionally detached, and a true answer is usually impossible. Although the positive response will encourage positive thinking which will help the person, the pendulum's answer may keep someone from obtaining proper medical attention. I have met only one person who is actually quite good with a pendulum for medical purposes, but since she is also a noted surgeon, she's the exception.

Do not let wishful thinking affect you.

In the early stages of the pendulum's use, it is important to understand that any question for which you have an **excessive** emotional interest in the outcome, when you are caught up in the heat of what is going on, may have a tainted answer. It is very easy to influence the pendulum with your own subjective desire for an outcome, with your own conscious opinion, unless you wait to detach yourself a little. Over time and with repeated use of the pendulum, you will learn how to put your mind in "neutral" more immediately.

This next exercise is extremely important. It will help close down all your thoughts and needs for a certain answer over the actual answer.

Exercise #5:

Think through a question first prior to holding the pendulum. Keep in mind, wherever it is these an-

swers come from, your questions are taken very literally. Word the question carefully, then pick up the pendulum, place it in the rest position, and then adopt the state of a child's innocence while asking yourself, "I wonder what the answer will be? I truly wonder what the answer will be?"

The above exercise must be worked on repeatedly if you are to receive true answers to the questions which matter most. Adopting the naive state of a "child's innocence" is the most crucial factor.

Going back to exercise #4 above, some people may wonder, why does this work? We know the pendulum can respond to questions about information buried deep within our mind and heart. It is an externalization of our intuition, but in this case of the unborn baby, how does our subconscious know something it cannot possibly know? Is our subconscious picking up subtle signals? Is our subconscious responding to something hormonal? Or on the other hand, perhaps the response of the pendulum has nothing to do with the subconscious. Is there something supernatural going on?

The "unborn sex test" goes centuries back in history. My great grandmother, born in Russia, had a remarkable accuracy rate with this procedure. She also had an intuition for anticipating the date of birth. She never tried to understand the reason. Long before The Beatles, she would say, "Let it be." And it is well known that for hundreds of years farmers have used the pendulum to sex eggs. Mention of the pendulum and its various uses even dates back to the Hebrews, Egyptians, Greeks, Druids and ancient Chinese as early as 2000 B.C. There are answers inquiring minds may never know, but some people claim the pendulum often functions as the vessel through which our intuition detects radiations from objects and conditions in other beings. On the other hand, scientist Emerson Pugh states: "If the human brain were so simple that we could understand it, we would be so simple that we wouldn't."

●

The following exercise lays necessary groundwork before attempting to find objects you have misplaced.

Exercise #6:

Stand at one end of a room with your back practically touching the wall. Ask the pendulum to find an object in the room for which you know the where-

abouts. The pendulum should begin to swing in the direction of the object. Draw an imaginary extension of the pendulum's line all the way across the room. Now stand 10 to 15 feet down the wall and ask the pendulum the same question. The pendulum again should begin to swing. Again draw an imaginary extension of this line across the room, and the spot of intersection with the first line will be the location of the object.

Do the above in several locations. You should also do it outdoors with nearby objects.

The following step requires a bit of your own absent-mindedness:

Exercise #7:

The next time you misplace something, locate it using the intersecting line method in exercise #6.

Also, patiently repeat this exercise dozens of times with a known object a friend hides for you, or you can go to your friend's home, stand in the kitchen and determine which cabinet contains the glasses and which drawer contains the silverware. If you have devoted the necessary attention to all of the above exercises, and if you have executed them in sequence, in time you will have success with exercise #7. From what I've seen, the delight and awe over the result causes either a yelp of excitement or stunned speechlessness. The greatest success, though, comes with things you have misplaced yourself, because obviously the pendulum helps to open memory banks deep in your subconscious.

Here are some important steps to remember while searching for your missing object when you're not even sure of its general whereabouts. Begin by asking **"YES-NO"** questions pertaining to general location, such as, "Are my keys located someplace other than in my house? Are my keys located inside my house? Are my keys upstairs? Are my keys downstairs? Are my keys in the dining room? Are my keys somewhere in the kitchen?" In this manner of **REDUCTION DEDUCTION** you will zero in on one particular room or area prior to employing the intersecting line procedure.

●

Now it is time to discuss the subject of unclear, confusing responses from the pendulum. Sometimes the pendulum will move in a straight line, then immediately start rotating in a circle, only to swing back into a straight line. Also, once in a while, the pendulum will have little or no movement. These are **"MAYBE"** responses.

A **"MAYBE"** response means the question cannot be answered definitively, and sometimes it means that you may be asking the wrong question. Some people ask, "Will I marry him?" when the question should be, "Should I marry him?" Also note that you may not want to hear the answer to a question of this nature. You may not be ready to make such a decision. It may not be the right time in the relationship. You may wish to ask, "Is this relationship one I should explore further?"

As mentioned before, a question like this implies an extreme emotional interest on the part of the asker. Here is another piece of useful information for queries of this type:

Exercise #8:

For questions which you have an extreme emotional interest in the outcome, after you receive your answer, follow it with this confirmation question: "Is this answer the TRUTH?" When you ask this question, it will be very easy to keep extraneous thoughts

from your mind and you will be focused. If the initial question is answered with a "YES" and the confirmation question is answered with a "NO," then the answer to the initial question is "NO." Thus, you have given your subconscious one more chance to speak the truth.

This exercise will increase in importance with the more advanced uses of the pendulum.

●

At this time, with what you have discovered and accomplished, even if you go no further into this exploration, you are aware of the power of the subconscious, you are aware of the existence of actual magic, you are aware of the transfer of information from the subconscious to the conscious mind, you are aware of how some things which seemed impossible can be made possible, and you are becoming aware of phenomena we don't usually consider in our everyday life. You have gone beyond simply dipping your feet into the ocean; you have put on the snorkeling mask and you are aware of what beauty lies just below the surface. Now if you wish, it is time to dive deeper.

Let's suppose you are about to interview for a job.

Exercise #9:

Privately, the night before, hold the pendulum in the rest position but do not ask questions. Instead, make statements. Make assertions such as the following: "I really want this job." Wait for the pendulum's response, then make another statement: "This career move will be good for me and my family." Again, note the pendulum's response. Other statements could be: "I am qualified for this job," or, "This company has a healthy work environment I will like." You will be verifying whether your subconscious agrees with your conscious. Following the interview (which, of course, is the time for you to find out as much about the company as they are about you) do this exercise again to compare with the pre-interview responses.

Supposing the first assertion above is answered with a **"NO"** response. How should you analyze this answer? Most likely it indicates you do not have the desire. The lack of desire could be the result of any one of a number of factors, most likely relating to one of the other assertions above. Maybe deep down you do not believe this job will be good for your family; for instance, it requires too much travel which keeps you away from them. Maybe you have some misgivings about the company. Maybe deep down you do not feel qualified; for instance, perhaps you have all the tools, you are qualified, but do not have the necessary confidence, or perhaps you really are not fully equipped to handle the tasks this job requires and/or you are not willing to learn, reach and work for a new and higher level.

All achievements begin with desire. If you don't desire it, it probably won't happen. Everything you see in the world, all the things and even all the children, began with desire. And desire often begins with necessity.

At this moment I am typing on a computer. Some of the great advancements in the development of the computer grew out of desire and necessity. The United States space program during the 1960s is one prime example. For millennia humanity has been fascinated by the heavens, and for years we had the desire to send people to our moon and bring them back safely. The desire to do so generated the creativity to overcome the obstacles. For instance, to travel beyond the gravity and atmosphere of our planet, the journey required infinitesimal course adjustments along the way to maintain the spacecraft on target. Such calculations would take a room full of mathematicians hours to complete meanwhile sending the mission further off course. So out of the necessity and desire to make the calculations in the few required moments, an on-board computer was developed for the trip. During the following ten years, relatively few people ever saw or operated a computer on their own, since one had to learn a specific computer language in order to operate it. Once again, it was desire which brought upon the creativity to make the computer more "user friendly," and it was desire which generated the ideas necessary to produce such machines at an affordable cost for home and small business use. And once some of these were on the market, other companies evolved out of a desire and necessity to make software and hardware that was even more affordable, more powerful, more helpful, more efficient and more complete.

Desire, desire, desire. Necessity breeds desire, and desire breeds invention. Necessity and desire are the mother and father of magical results.

Even the beginning of our universe began with desire. This author believes desire is the thing in all matter which creates new matter. Desire may be the smallest particle of all, smaller than an atom, smaller than a quark, yet it has the largest results. It is the end point of infinity, and it is the beginning of infinity. Like the mind, it cannot be seen, but it is there. It is the force behind all existence.

At this time I want you to think about what you desire more than anything else. Sit yourself in a quiet place and decide upon the one thing you would yearn for above everything else. You may have several needs and wants, but for what I am about to share, you must hold one desire above all the others.

One person I know wished for a certain salary, another for a luxury automobile, someone else for a specific home, another for a particular job promotion, another for a loving relationship, someone else for a trip to a location in the Orient. A former associate of mine desired a move to a Western state, while another friend's supreme desire was for a more fit body. Notice these were all elevated, yet reasonable desires. Needless to say, with the use of the enclosed information, all of these desires came to fruition.

Magic is defined as making something possible that at first does not seem possible. Do not confuse this principle with the stage magician. The tuxedoed stage performer will snap his fingers and something will appear. It is make-believe, an illusion. Real magic makes your desire appear, but since it is real, it rarely occurs in an instant. The great difference is that real magic does not transpire in the snap of a finger. Desires take weeks, months or years to materialize. Sending astronauts Neil Armstrong, Michael Collins and Buzz Aldrin to the moon took a decade, saving the bald eagle from extinction took more than a decade, and in the eighteenth century, making democracy a reality was a monumental dream which took lives and decades to achieve. A tree isn't grown in a day. A seed is planted. Attention, nourishment and time are given. Then the seed germinates, grows and blooms. That is true enchantment.

There have always been a few people who know this power, and now we will learn the power of nourishing your desire so it too will blossom and thrive.

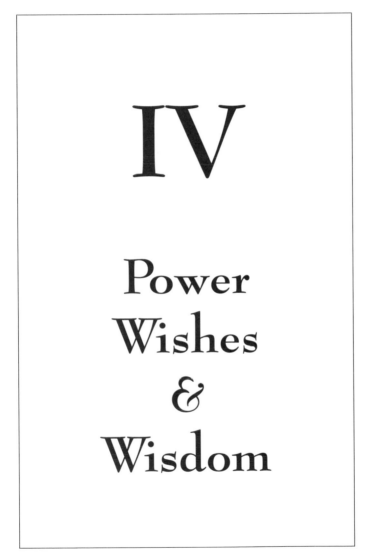

IV

Power
Wishes
&
Wisdom

IV

Power, Wishes & Wisdom

Desire makes a moment matter. And, all matter is made by moments of desire.

•

We have talked about the transfer of subconscious information to the conscious mind. Now we will learn about transferring your conscious thoughts and desires to your subconscious.

Each heart has a limited number of beats. The pulses run out way before eternity. In comparison to all the time that preceded us and all the time to follow, existence becomes brief.

Chronologically, we are somewhere in the middle of it all. There were eons before us and eons to follow.

There are lessons in limits. There is reason for this absence of eternity in life on earth. We are ultimately powerless against this fate, but we do have another kind of power, another kind of control, and it's a supreme power. It is a power over the moment. It is a power over all the moments within the span of a life. We either stretch them, we feel these moments, or we diminish them, even ignore them. The positive power is in the former. Each moment in a day we either feel and expand, or we compress it and pass it by, hardly even noticing its contents.

The more moments we behold, the more powerful we become. The more we taste, hear, smell, feel and see, the more vital and dynamic we become. Life stretches a little further toward eternity. Desire makes a moment matter. Life takes on fuller meaning.

All the senses must take part in the experience. Occasionally, the sense of sight may be the exception. We see enough already. For most, no matter how acute or diminished, sight seems to dull the other senses. It influences us too much, so much so it often overrides our other faculties. We aren't true to them.

Do you merely eat or do you truly taste? Close your eyes as the bite of food enters your lips. Keep them closed while you roll it around your tongue. Feel the texture, then slowly chew. Swallow with ease, then taste the aftertaste. Smell the lingering aroma. Hear your satisfied breath. Clear your palate with water and revel in the memory!

When you close your eyes, the other senses become more alert. The more alert the senses, the more you savor. The more you savor, the more you live.

●

All matter is made by moments of desire. The seeds in the ground **will** their way through hard turf to life. The baby robin **wills** its way through the wall of the egg to life on earth, not to mention the mother and father who made the fertile egg from **their** moments of will and desire. Necessity and desire sire success.

By now, you have thought about the one thing you yearn for, your one reasonable desire that stands above all others. Hopefully, it stands far above and was readily apparent to you. The more burning the desire, and the more it makes you toss and turn, and the more it is fully wanted, the more probable its attainment. Actually, there are only a few basic desires in the world. Your desire has something to do with travel, health, education, love, career, nature or money. These are the categories for just about every human wish, want, and need.

Here is the science of making your desire a reality. Be sure you have an understanding and facility with the previous exercises, then follow these guidelines precisely:

Exercise #10:

Think of a short phrase of about two to seven words which represents this desire. The shorter, the better. That is to say, the more precise and to the point, the more focussed you will be. Hold the pendulum in the rest position. Out loud, slowly repeat the phrase several times. The pendulum will respond. You should receive a positive response which will verify the intensity of the desire and whether it is truly the one thing you wish for more than anything else.

On the other hand, if the pendulum moves in a circle, you may wish to rethink your stated desire.

Also, consider the possibility you may be content with your position in life, or you may not have a desire great enough on which to focus. There may not be the necessity. Another more likely reason for the negative response is that you have some fear of tapping the truth in your subconscious; you are blocking some deeply hidden want or need. It is also possible you may not feel you deserve what you desire. You may have to do some self-exploration with your pendulum, asking your subconscious questions to get to the root of the reason. You may have to wait days or months or longer until some wish truly burns in your gut. If the above is the case, fulfill this exercise:

Exercise #11:

Hold the pendulum in the rest position and repeat some positive affirmations, some endorsements of your value. Speak to yourself with confident statements such as "I am strong," "I am loved," "I am a good person," "I am happy," "I am open to what my heart holds," "I am worthy of my wish," "I am deserving of my desire."

This exercise of affirmations works, and it is helpful for everyone. Employ exercise #11 as a vitamin for the soul, a dose of vim and vigor for your confidence.

Once you have a definitive, positive response to the phrase back in exercise #10, write the phrase in a number of places. Write it on a small piece of paper and put it in your wallet or purse. Write it in your date book under Monday of each week. Write it on a slip of paper and put it in your sock drawer. Write it on a business card and use it as a book mark for a book you are reading. Put this phrase in at least four or five frequented places. Post-It Notes™ are good for this too. As you have undoubtedly surmised, by seeing the desire at various times during each day, you will help to embed this conscious thought into your subconscious. You are continually feeding and reminding your subconscious.

Here is the important part:

Exercise #12:

Begin each morning by taking one of the cards or papers and hold your pendulum over the phrase for

3 to 5 minutes and think "YES." Think a definitive "YES." Watch the pendulum begin to swing back and forth, back and forth. Focus on the pendulum. Keep thinking "YES." Watch it swing in a greater, longer line back and forth, back and forth, to and fro, concentrating on the phrase beneath, thinking "YES," thinking of the phrase, making a clear mental picture of your wish, thinking "YES" again, presenting the phrase as the pendulum continues to swing, visualizing the mental image of your desire, always thinking "YES."

By loading the subconscious with your desire, by pouring in your wish until the subconscious is filled to the brim, the subconscious will go to work to make it a reality. The subconscious is extremely receptive to positive propositions. In the beginning, you will have no inkling as to how the results are to happen. Just leave it to the subconscious. Doors will begin to open and new avenues will appear. But even more, ideas will come to you as to how to get to your destination. Write these ideas down immediately. Always carry a note pad or some type of planner with you. Write everything that pops into your mind. And follow-up on these notions.

Another good time to do this twelfth exercise is prior to bedtime. Most important, do it in private.

Do not share your desire with anyone else. Keep it to yourself. The more you tell, the more the forces at work are dissipated. The less you guard your desire, the more you lose your bond with the subconscious. You don't have to inform anyone. Others will see the difference in you; your progress will be obvious all along the journey.

A remarkable outcome from the daily use of this exercise is the resulting detachment it gives you from the future and from the past. This freedom is necessary to achieve an ambition. During those 3 to 5 minutes of the exercise you will be completely attached to the goal, to the outcome, to the potential of the future; but following the exercise, for the rest of the day you will be detached from the future, disengaged from the goal, and you will confidently exist solely in the present moment and the work at hand. What is more, you will be full of energy, but you will not be tense. Your focus on the tasks at hand will be strong and determined, but you will not have anxiety.

This exercise helps to relinquish worry and fear, yet it provides calm determination. Tension, anxiety, worry and fear all get in the way of the natural forces that work to make a desire a reality; and by eliminating them, by detaching all the tomorrows from today, and by detaching all the yesterdays from today, exercise #12 allows you to effortlessly proceed, it allows you to be absorbed in the moment, to even lose awareness of time, and it allows the future to take care of itself.

Continue this exercise until the desire is realized, and reread what was written about real magic in the previous chapter. With the science presented here, some progress will be seen almost immediately, **but full materialization of the desire takes time.** It is a road, an adventure. Revel in the journey! Revere the moment! Expand each moment! Climb through the moment! Praise yourself for each step forward! Picture the destination each day! Believe in the power deep within you, the power of the invisible!

The forces of the invisible have been proven to you throughout your life. Everything we do in life, each action and each breath, is accomplished with one of the oldest, greatest unseen machines. Scientists and surgeons have all seen brains, but no one has seen a mind. It is there, yet it is invisible. The subconscious is part of that machine. Nurture it. Feed it. Fill it and fulfill it.

•

Describing how others have succeeded with these techniques somehow seems out of place since it may be best to find out for yourself. Nevertheless, a few outstanding examples will be mentioned. Following my presentations I am continually approached by people with their experiences of tapping their subconscious. Some of these stories may be innocently exaggerated, but the following are among the incidents that have checked out to be true and accurate.

One fellow told me of a luxury car he wished to own someday. He put a picture of that automobile on his desk at work and several times a day he would put his forefinger on it, just touching it for a moment every so often. Several years later he not only owned that car but he had met his wife and had increased his expendable income enough to also purchase her a fancy mode of transportation.

Under the "Fairy Tales Do Come True, It Can Happen to You" category, a divorced woman recently related her experience of visiting the place of her ancestry. It had been a wish of hers for many years, but going to Ireland with two children was a costly trip for her means and she wanted them to share the experience. She had been told about feeding the subconscious by someone who attended one of my talks, and her daily diligence with these intuition exercises helped her to come up with ideas for a part-time business operated out of her home which earned the money for the voyage. What you will discover, as she did, is that one desire will often flow into another. During her first few days in Ireland, she decided her new desire was to someday meet a loving, caring husband, someone with whom she could share her life. Again, she began to work with her subconscious. Whether it was curious chance, the power of the pendulum or both, on the plane flight home she met a widowed Irish gentleman on his way to New York for business. At home, he too had two children. Now, three years later, they are one family living in Ireland.

Many business executives tell me of how their office walls are filled with sayings and quotes which have served to positively fuel their subconscious. One executive in particular told me how his long hours of work never had much of a pay-off in his early days.

He always felt like he was spinning his wheels in mud. When the mud got deeper than he could manage, he began "talking" to his subconscious. He began using mental images and verbalizing his desires, writing down his wish to move up the ladder. In fact, he put a toy ladder, borrowed from his son, on his desk as a symbol. He still worked the many hours, but soon the hours were organized in such a way that his productivity doubled, sometimes tripled. Before long he was coming up with ideas and solutions to problems which his company had faced for years. His abilities were recognized, and he moved up the ranks. Political jealousy eventually forced him out of the firm, but again he put his subconscious powers to work for him. Two months later he was hired by a major telecommunications manufacturer and in the ensuing years became their Chief Executive Officer.

Since he was a young boy, golfer Tiger Woods' desire was to one day break the records of legend Jack Nicklaus. He may not have written phrases on cards, but he did something similar. He taped Nicklaus's press clippings to his bed posts and headboard. Yes, Woods was a prodigy blessed with natural gifts, and like Mozart he had a father who schooled and guided him in his craft. There are many reasons for his success, but don't doubt for a minute that the Nicklaus images above his pillow didn't serve to fuel the subconscious of Tiger Woods and keep him on track for his paramount achievements. He saw Nicklaus before he closed his eyes at dusk, and he saw the Nicklaus standard when he opened his eyes at dawn.

Famous hotelier Conrad Hilton carried a picture of New York's Waldorf-Astoria Hotel in his pocket for almost twenty-five years until finally, in 1949, his goal came true and he owned the property. Hilton was both a master of listening to his hunches and a master of feeding his subconscious with his dreams.

Another way to look at this technique is to consider what the advertising and marketing firms do for the products they represent. They are continually presenting images and phrases over and over again until the product, its uses, its benefits, its ability to solve a problem, and its ability to bring gratification are ingrained in our subconscious. We are not always thinking about soap, but if the marketing of a soap product is successful, when we walk down the soap aisle in the store, the advertised impressions and concepts lying dormant in our subconscious now come to the fore with a feeling of familiarity and comfort when we see that particular soap brand on the shelf, and thus we are more compelled to grab it, throw it in the shopping cart and buy it.

In a similar way, exercises #10 and #12 are accomplishing the same feat. You are "marketing" your desire and its fulfillment to yourself. You are continually feeding your subconscious with your goal. You are making the aspiration a part of all of you. The work required to achieve the desire will become habit; it may become almost effortless, the ideas will evolve, and the desire will be fact.

Do you need a pendulum to make a desire a reality? Of course not. As in some of these examples, people successfully employ this technique without it. Most people don't even know what it is. But, for those of us who do, the pendulum tool will focus our attention, intention and determination to an even greater degree than without it. One can get from Boston to Denver by walking, but there are more expedient ways to travel.

In addition to these exercises, at some point through this process, you must also picture the desire in your mind as if it is already achieved. Imagine yourself in the position of successfully attaining the particular desire. Imagine it in as much detail as possible. Imagine your state of mind. Imagine everything about yourself and your surroundings. Even imagine the elation and pride of reaching the plateau. **If you can imagine the change without it seeming strange, the change will exchange with the present.**

The great Martin Luther King, Jr. employed the same techniques to help others realize his and their dream of racial equality. Perceptions, actions and laws were different until there appeared this man of great conviction and belief in the idea of equality, a man who also had the great ability to feed the collective subconscious of the country with these just principles, a man who with the great force of his words and elocution impelled thousands of people from all races and creeds to nonviolently march and chant with him for long-overdue change in the society. "We shall overcome" and "I have a dream" are just two of the phrases and images that sold his ideas. And, in almost every speech, King would tell people to **IMAGINE** the day when **ALL** people are "judged not by the color of their skin but by the content of their character." Part of his magic was to continually feed his audience with the end result, the attained dream, the fulfilled wish. Many people had been beaten and kicked for years. Many people had given up. Many people were in a mind-set that the way it is is the way it should be, and there was nothing they could do about it. Yet, by repeating key phrases, and by repeatedly petitioning people to see the future of freedom and to feel what it would be like to be "free at last" by employing this technique, the dream (or at least a significant part of the dream) was made a reality.

Imagine the change without it seeming strange. Imagine it so it becomes familiar.

Dozens of men and women have told me of their desire to change careers or to receive a promotion. They talk about the change in their way of perceiving the forces of the heart and mind, learning to tap and keep tapping their power no matter what gets in their way. The results are astounding. For the most part these people are not only receiving what they desire, but in the process they are discovering what type of vocation gives them a sense of purpose and gratification. There may be nothing more important in life. Monday is the day people return to work, work most people dread, and it is no accident, by current medical statistics, more heart attacks occur on Monday than on any other day. Stress from work may be the leading hindrance to enchanted living, and according to these findings it is a leading hindrance to living, period.

So it is valuable to develop a set of personal commandments, so to speak, by which one lives, with the goal of making life healthy, simple and magical. In addition to self-evident moralities, one's own religious beliefs, and inalienable rights of humankind, it is helpful to organize and decide on some personal basic means through which one will attain contentment and give fulfillment.

●

Here is a guide of **17 common, sensible, simple, yet for some reason, often unobserved means to gratification.** They may seem obvious, but do not be oblivious to the first four:

1) Pursue the work you love to do.
2) Seek the people you love to be with.

*3) **Find the place where you love to live.***
*4) **Appreciate each of these discoveries.***

Work, relationships, surroundings and appreciation. With the former, discover the one thing, be it vocation or avocation, which in your heart you know you do well, you know you are willing to cultivate, and you sense fulfills a purpose. It is known by philosopher Joseph Campbell as "finding your bliss." Whether it becomes a full-time or part-time endeavor, you must discover your talent, your forte, your gift; each human being has at least one special aptitude, one unique interest. Often it will be something which causes you to lose track of time, something which can completely envelop you. When you find it, you must develop it with devotion. Many of the enclosed exercises will help in this pursuit.

If you must concentrate on only one aspect of life, this is it. The others will follow naturally in time, especially when you keep in mind that as for relationships and surroundings, your existence and growth is defined and influenced in large part by the place around you and the people who surround you.

Of the first three means above, when you have at least two of the three in order and appreci-

ate what you have, you are living a fairly gratified and reasonably sane life.

Along the way, even if you have not yet found the ultimate work, relationships or location, the determined act of finding these necessities can also bring gratification. The unearthing process itself can and should bring joy. **Relish the task.** Often it is not the destination, but the journey toward the destination that matters. Sports teams who put all the pieces together and have that once-in-a-generation magical season often are surprised to feel an emptiness after reaching their ultimate goal of winning a championship. "We're here, now what?" Often, they look back over the year and then realize it was the moments along the long path, the challenging voyage to the new shore which brought the most exhilaration and lasting memories. The arrival must now bring a new and different kind of satisfaction. And usually, following a rest, that satisfaction is in setting a new aspiration.

5) *Find at least one time in life to have a close, communicative relationship with an animal.*

There are few better feelings than hugging a pet. There are few greater examples of living in the moment than the spirit of the puppy or kitten. There are few purer bonds than that which can be established between human and animal. Most animals do not have our vocal abilities or quite the same mental reasoning faculties, but they have other faculties and abilities which on those terms make us inferior. A dog's sense of smell is several hundred times greater than the human's. The leaping and landing skill of the cat, jungle and domestic, makes Michael Jordan and Mikhail Baryshnikov seem grounded. And above all, do not underestimate the intelligence, awareness and sensibilities of many dog and cat breeds, and of innumerable other creatures on the planet. They have astuteness, cognizance, feelings and even moralities which only pet owners, animal observers and some scientists comprehend and appreciate.

6) Find time to help someone in need.

All truly unconditional giving ironically comes full circle. Give unconditionally and you will receive. Of course, if you think about the giving coming back to you, then you are not giving unconditionally. Pure giving for the benefit of someone else is a rarity but a necessity.

When you give, magical things happen. You become even more aware of your feelings. And when you profoundly feel, you develop a hunger. And when you hunger, you will seek. And when you seek, you will find. And when you find, you will grow. And when you grow, you will prosper. And when you prosper, you will give.

7) Find moments to breathe with awareness of the fact you are breathing.

Be aware of the things we do instinctively, especially this most basic, life-sustaining process of taking in and letting out oxygen. Every so often in each day consider how you are breathing. Notice everything. **The depth, pace and length of your breath has bearing on the depth, pace and length of your life,** and it affects the transfer of information from the intuitive mind to the conscious mind and vice versa.

8) Concentrate.

To attain anything, you must devote eight hours a day to concentrated work. Focussed, uninter-rupted action is a key to productivity. Some of us are programmed naturally to do this. Whether the ability is genetic, influenced, learned, or part of all three, if you have trouble keeping your attention fixed on the tasks at hand, and you have already unsuccessfully attempted a number of things to improve this capacity on your own, you may wish to seek some professional help. The ability to truly concentrate is a difficult thing for more people than you would think, so do not feel alone in this matter if you are one of them. Fortunately, in the latter part of the twentieth century and beyond, there are some solutions to this hindrance. Some people accomplish in a day what others do in a week, and they do it with time left for socializing and rest. Strive to be one of them.

9) Be there.

Go, go, go. Go where the work is. Be near the opportunities. As an obvious and simple example, if your career is acting and you desire to work in major motion pictures, relocating to Los Angeles would serve your wish better than to remain at your home town in central Idaho. Likewise, if you are a farmer and want to grow oranges, you would not till 500 acres in Minnesota. If you wish to find a foreign product to import, most likely you will require visits to other lands. Find where the opportunities exist, then be there.

If it is money you want, you must associate yourself with those who have it, with those who know how to acquire it, and with those who have the authority to spend it. This may sound blatant, but here too, if you want it, you must go there. For instance, if you are a computer software salesperson and you know that the C.E.O. of a particular company is the one with the final say, it is a waste of time attempting to convince the vice presidents and the middle managers. The same is true for the sale of just about any product— you must present yourself to the decision-makers.

10) Talk to the elderly and truly hear their story.

We are a world of youth worshipers, but the people wisest about life are those who have lived it. Their meaningful memories become even more vivid for them in the denouement of life. Truly absorb the content of their thoughts and stories. Truly listen for the feeling behind the words. From the things you will hear, you may learn to savor and expand the brief minutes of youth, you may learn to work smarter, you may learn to love. Combine your innocence with their experience and the result is magic. They can see the past; you now may see the future.

11) Ask questions.

Ask and listen. People respond and connect with us when we ask sincere questions and hear what they have to say.

Why is this so? People want to be liked and loved. How do we show we like others? We show it by our interest in them. How do we show our interest? We show it by asking questions. **Just like the pendulum, people respond when we ask questions.** Just like our subconscious, people connect with us when we ask questions with an open frame of mind.

Curiously and wonderfully, you may have noticed in working with the pendulum, the more we ask, the more our subconscious feels loved. When we work with the pendulum, our confidence and self-love grows. As with the subconscious, the same is true for interaction between people. The more a person feels heard, the more one feels appreciated; and the more we are appreciated, the more we are connected with others.

12) *Touch and connect.*

A very profitable small hotel in San Francisco achieved its success in part by touching. Although the lobby atmosphere is cozy and fairly elegant, the rooms are average. Yet it is booked every night of the week and people return time after time. The owner was interviewed on television one night and, when asked about his secret for success, he mentioned that he makes a point of touching many patrons with a friendly pat on the back, a handshake, or a sincere touch on the arm.

I've observed him and his doormen in person, and in a natural, non-sexual, friendly manner they make contact with just about everyone. Touching, in the right way, makes people feel welcome, makes them feel at home, and makes them feel at ease, like one of the family. **The comfort they feel is a result of something very subconscious, because the touch is so natural and brief. It is something no one CONSCIOUSLY recalls, but their subconscious remembers, and that is what brings them back.**

Yes, there are a few people in the world who do not want their space invaded, and that's fine. If you are aware and sensitive, you can notice them and respect the distance they require. But always keep in mind, if done in a genuine, appropriate and unaffected manner, most people respond positively to this incredibly basic form of connection.

Concerning touch on a deeper level, when a being feels connected with others, the mind and body of the being are calmed and soothed; the being is more alert, more active, more responsive and more capable.

Observe two kennels with dogs whose owners have gone on vacation. The kennel that routinely massages and pets the animals will have owners return to find their pets relatively unstressed and happier than at the kennel where the dogs are just stuck in a cage with little contact.

Go to a hospital. It is proven that regularly massaged premature infants gain weight faster and will leave the hospital sooner than non-massaged premature infants. The benefits of massage for practically all beings are numerous. In short, touch stimulates the brain. We have millions of receptors in our skin (several thousand in one fingertip alone) which send messages along the spinal cord to the brain which then produces endorphins which then reduce pain; plus stress hormone levels are lowered, immunities are enhanced, and the vagus cranial nerve is stimulated to positively influence several bodily functions.

If you have children, hug them, pat their backs, and maybe even rub their feet on occasion. If you are married or in a relationship, learn to thoroughly massage each other. If you are alone, treat yourself to a professional massage by a skillful massage therapist. Touch is not taboo. Touch stabilizes society. **Touch is a synonym for peace.**

13)   Write, write, write.

Keep a private journal. You do not have to write a lot, you do not have to write with artful elegance, but make a point of writing at least four or five phrases each day. Write a thought about the past, write a thought about the present, write your ideas (just as mentioned earlier in this chapter), write about a dream, write about a concern, and no matter what, always write about the things for which you are grateful. Even on the worst day, there are always people, places, circumstances, deeds or events for which you can give thanks. Write them; you will soon right all else.

Equally important, whether from the distant past or from the present moment, if angry about something, write it out. Troubles will tend to flow from your head and heart, through your body, through your hand and onto your paper, releasing the tension, softening the ire, bringing revelation, and developing understanding.

Write it out and you get it out. Express it with your pen and the problem may not bother you again. If you've never written before, just do it. If you've written some, do it some more.

The pen is mighty.
Your words are gold.
From head and body,
release the hold.

14) *Find a balance of exercise, rest and nourishment.*

Physically and metabolically, we are not all exactly the same. There is an experimentation process we each must go through to find out the amounts and kinds of sustenance, activities and relaxation which make each of us feel right and well. There is a trial and error approach to what and how much we eat, to what kind of and how much bodily exertion we do, and to how much we sleep, rejuvenate and meditate. Our search for these answers is aided by this current era of extensive theories, studies and facts about health, combined with our own intuitive common sense. Here too, the pendulum will be of assistance, especially when used in conjunction with common knowledge.

At the least, walk. Our bodies are made for walking. And bear in mind these three apparent truisms:

    a) The active, fit body sustains an alert mind.
    b) It's not only that you rest, but how you rest.
    c) All things in moderation.

15) *Organize.*

Your mind is in order when your surroundings are in order. Open a closet and throw out the clutter, go through a pile of papers and keep only what is necessary, peruse your purse or wallet and jettison the junk.

Paraphrasing the observer George Carlin, he says, "STUFF. Everyone owns a pile of STUFF. If you took away all the houses you would just see piles of STUFF. And when we go on vacation, we come back with a suitcase filled with more STUFF to add to our STUFF."

So (keeping to the rule of moderation) go ahead, have one closet where you stuff your stuff, but overall, the great majority of your surroundings should contain only the stuff that is necessary, organized and uncluttered.

Chaos enslaves. Order emancipates.

16) Read biographies.

There is no greater lesson in achievement than to study how others achieved. Earlier, we mentioned Milton Hershey. For twenty years of his adult life he failed at numerous businesses, but he believed beyond any doubt he would make it big at something some day. He did not succumb to his defeats, and finally, in his forties, he began selling chocolate. The rest is history. His example of hard-sought attainment and resulting philanthropy is useful for everyone.

In addition to biographies, one should continually seek the companionship of many books, fiction and nonfiction. We spoke earlier in this chapter about the use of the pendulum to generate ideas to help make your wishes come to fruition. I guarantee, if you read, the ideas will come even faster and in greater number. Just about every book has one or two useful ideas applicable to your own work and life. From the centuries, we have inherited a wealth of wisdom inked between the covers of outstanding books. The information is there for a reason; spend the wealth.

And finally, as mentioned, an essential step toward serenity and enchantment is the following:

17) Regard, observe and understand real magic.

Explore actual magic, not trickeries, but tangible extraordinary special events in your life, whether observed from afar or intimately experienced, moments you want to stretch and savor and wish could last forever, because **the act of not taking an extraordinary moment for granted is the act of seeing and experiencing real magic, true enchantment.**

Desire makes that moment matter. And, all matter is made by moments of desire.

V

Creation

V

Creation

At several points between the ages of about 7 and 70 we think about meaning in life, the essence of existence.

Some people are content to live a stagnant pattern. Work, eat, rest; work, eat, rest; buy insurance; work, eat, rest; retire, die, let someone collect. It could all be that simple, but one morning during the routine, perhaps especially in this era, some of us awake, asking if there is more, searching for purpose, exploring a rationale for the reality, pondering the tangible like composer David Byrne: "Letting the days go by, let the water hold me down. . . . You may find yourself in a beautiful house with a beautiful wife. . . . You may ask yourself, 'Well, how did I get here?'"

We rise and look out at the day with yearnings and questions.

Either there are no answers, or, while there may not be an exact answer, there may be a key to the puzzle.

This solution is found in the very thing that started it all, creation itself.

Not long ago, through some explosive feat, our universe, world and lives were created. So to speak, life was made and developed with some extraordinary foresight and invention. There may be other plans and missions for us, but it seems the prime purpose of life is to create. We were created, therefore it may be our mission to return the gift, to reciprocate with extraordinary creations of our own making.

Do unto the world as was done for us. Act as Godly as we possibly can. Imitate God as best we can. We as humans, with our gift of intelligence, have the ability to imagine, to solve and to conceive.

The lesson may be to think always in terms of creation. It does not matter so much whether you create a piece of needlepoint or a law to improve the community. It does not matter whether you create a finger painting or a garden of vegetables. It matters not whether you create a simple poem or a solution to a problem at your place of work. Whether your creation is a warm, loving home or a child to raise in that home, all responsible creations are acts of reciprocation, deeds of thanks for our own being.

As it turns out, these creations are also the greatest source of fulfillment, and they are the main means toward immortality, toward leaving a lasting memory of our hour on earth, toward making our life extend beyond our life.

Perpetually think in terms of creation. If you are not creating, you should be admiring creation. If you are not admiring creation, you should be taking time to contemplate what needs a little recreating, a little fixing, and what can be made better in the world, beyond the globe, in your life and in your work. Creative people are the successful people, the enlightened ones.

Think eternally in terms of creation, invention and discovery. Break the barrier of mortality. Then, through life you will have energy, vitality and meaning. And at the end of life, miraculously, you will die without dying. Bodies die, but creation always grows.

VI

Free-Form Subconscious Communication

VI

Free-Form Subconscious Communication

Step by step we have learned how to make specific inquiries to the intuitive part of the mind. We have worked with a defined language between the conscious and subconscious. The pendulum is well-suited for this type of question and answer technique. In addition, we have worked with a method of feeding a desire to the subconscious so that the subconscious can go to work for us in making the desire a reality.

Sometimes though, we do not know what question to ask; we may be caught in a rut concerning our growth and needs. Other times, we may wish to explore the parts of the mind hidden from us in everyday life; we seek to find our secret longings and ambitions. Or, at times we may wish to heighten our creativity.

In these cases it may be more effective not to limit or define the areas for subconscious exploration. Although the pendulum may be used, there is an even more productive technique for this particular task. It is a method I call **Free-Form Subconscious Communication.**

The basic idea is to put yourself in a "meditative" state of mind, empty of all conscious thoughts, and allow the subconscious to communicate with the conscious without asking any specific questions. The purpose here is to allow the "hidden" parts of the mind decide what images, thoughts or memories are important to know and to bring them to the fore.

You may employ this technique in two ways: to recall a memory, or to come up with ideas.

For each, you will need to obtain a goblet, cup or glass. A receptacle that is a little more unusual than the norm or has an interesting exterior pattern is best for this purpose. An old teacup that belonged to your grandmother, a beautiful cut crystal vase, or a special wine glass will work. Fill it with a red wine or any dark, rich liquid (see **Sample Photographs**).

To recall a past memory, do the following:

Exercise #13:

In a quiet, comfortable, candle-lit setting with absolutely no distractions, sit yourself in the middle of the room at an empty table covered with a white tablecloth. Place the goblet in front of you and fill it. With good posture and each hand gently resting on each of your thighs, close your eyes. Slowly inhale through your nose, then slowly exhale through your mouth. Repeat the gentle breathing pattern for several minutes, all the while clearing your mind of all conscious thoughts as if you are exhaling them out of your body. For a moment, open your eyes and stare down into the goblet continuing to breathe in the same manner. Then close your eyes again and deliberately recite 3 or 4 times out loud the following quatrain:

> *Upon you, round cup, my vision is cast*
> *To bring up what's lost, a memory past;*
> *So that the eyes and mind again see*
> *A symbol, an image, now conscious in me.*

Open your eyes gazing down into the contents of the goblet and be prepared for a surprise. An old, forgotten memory will come into your consciousness.

To create and foster ideas and images that are not necessarily memories, do the following:

Exercise #14:

Utilize the same procedure in Exercise #13 above, substituting this quatrain:

Within you, round cup, my view is in place
To bring up a thought, an idea, a trace;
So that the eyes and mind start to see
Impressions and notions now open to me.

Open your eyes and gaze into the contents of the goblet. An idea, an image, some indication will propose itself to your conscious mind.

By description alone, it is hard to imagine the impact of this technique until you actually try it. Most important, you must have a tranquil setting and a relaxed body. The results are exceptional following a session of physical exercise and a calming bath.

This concept is not new. It has been practiced throughout the world for centuries. Other forms of this idea include the crystal ball and dream analysis. Although often considered hokum, crystal balls have been used for many years as a focal point to open the mind to hidden ideas with the intent of receiving images which are analyzed for their meanings. While a crystal ball is a beautiful object, it is often more distracting than helpful and usually does not encourage free-form communication, not only because of the dubious implications associated with it, but because of its ability to refract light and reflect physical images from the room in which you are sitting.

Many people feel their dreams offer us the same possibilities. Dreams are also a free-form indication of the contents in the subconscious. They may be helpful, but since we are not awake when they occur, most of us remember few of our dreams, forget important details and often have difficulty telling if the dream is significant. The goblet allows you to tap the subconscious in the same non-directive manner, but even though you are in a meditative state, you are doing it while cognizant.

Since we are on the subject, if you are interested in dream analysis, it is significant to mention the goblet and the pendulum can be tools to help clarify and find meanings in dreams you may believe are significant. For instance, on occasion, the use of the goblet will recall a past dream. Then, with the pendulum, you can ask defining questions about the recollected image. Also, if you awake one morning with a dream fresh in your mind, you can utilize the pendulum to illuminate hidden meanings, or you can immediately employ the goblet technique to bring about a symbol, thought or message which may be helpful in analyzing the dream.

Of all the techniques for Free-Form Subconscious Communication, the goblet seems most applicable for an unstructured search. It works well for many reasons. One reason may be the connotations and quintessence of the cup and its contents. In many traditions the cup and the grape represent the emotions. They represent our non-intellectual side and thus are suitable for this non-directive approach with the subconscious.

My first exposure to this phenomenon was at a dinner party. One of the guests, a writer, was preoccupied and not at all convivial through cocktails and most of dinner. During one of the latter courses I noticed her staring for a few minutes into her wine glass with a glazed look when she suddenly jumped from her chair, went to her purse, wrote a note on a little pad of paper, then returned relaxed and now sociable. Later in the evening I spoke with her about this change that came over her and her look of revelation when she left the table. She told me she had been struggling over her next book idea when suddenly, while looking into the glass, she saw a vision of the heroine. I asked if her ideas ever came to her in this manner before, and she then realized this occurrence was not the first time. There were a couple of other similar instances, but until I pointed out her actions, she hadn't payed much attention to what she was actually doing when these ideas popped into her head.

A few months later at a dinner party of my own, I did an experiment after the table was cleared. I brought out fresh glasses (intended solely for this purpose) and filled them with some merlot or grape juice, then directed everyone what to do. The use of the unusual setting with candles, an antique tablecloth, and the motivational poem really helped to set the scene properly. As I watched person after person surprise themselves by the information their "goblets" were able to bring forth, even in such a lighthearted party setting, I began to realize the goblet's power to stimulate ideas or to get in touch with forgotten desires, dreams and memories. When finished, we simultaneously drank the contents of our glasses.

In the following year I tutored dozens of people on how to conduct this method of Free-Form Subconscious Communication, and along the way I honed and developed the technique and quatrains. The end product is in these pages.

The results are impressive: A business executive came up with a memory of an investment gone bad which compelled him to do more research into a current investment he was considering. He avoided the same pitfall. After employing the goblet, a friend of mine saw a childhood incident concerning an argument she had with her older brother. It led her to realize why she had hidden resentment toward him, and it gave her some keys as to why she was having some difficulties with her current boyfriend. An artist had a memory of a family trip to the Grand Canyon revived, which inspired his next painting. A vision of a broken-down car came to a young pharmaceutical salesperson just before embarking on a five-state sales trip. Her car just had a tune-up two months prior, but a major breakdown was avoided when she took the auto to the shop to be checked out. An engaged couple, each using the goblet on their own, decided on a honeymoon location after a vision of the same island came to both of them. A man, totally at a loss as to what to buy his wife for her birthday, brought forth a memory about her desire for a leather jacket.

The goblet gaze is a special tool. Use it properly, and with it, parts of the mind will come out of hiding. They will peer out. You may see the past, you may see the present, you may see an idea, and at times, you may see the future.

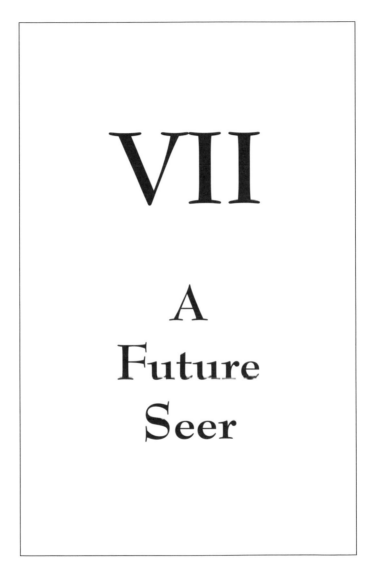

VII

A
Future
Seer

VII

A Future Seer

At every point in time, the future is uncertain. No psychic, no futurist, no scientist, nor any prognosticator can predict with absolute precision any of the next moments. That is the way it is, and it should not be a frustration. It is the way it should be. What will happen exactly where, when and how is a necessary mystery.

If certainty were a fact, there would be no beauty, there would be no enchantment. That is a law of our universe.

If certainty were a fact, there would be no desire. With no desire, there would be no need for creation. And with no creation, we and everything would not exist.

On the other hand, while you cannot see the fine details of what is to come, there exists the ability to receive impressions of future potentials. Regardless of the amount of this ability you presume you possess, you can develop even greater prescience, a more sensitive anticipation of what lies ahead.

This is especially true with your own future, with the things you have a hand in, and quite possibly, with the future of those closest to you.

To accomplish this skill, you must undertake what is, for many of us, the tall task of extinguishing almost all fears and hesitations about tomorrow and the following moments. In addition, you must combine and sift two abilities:

1) **With the subconscious, you must have an intuitive feel for what is to come;**

2) **With the conscious, you must comprehend the future consequence of the present circumstance.**

To some degree, you do these already. There have been numerous situations where you have anticipated the consequences of your actions, or have awakened in the morning with a feeling about the day to come. These abilities can be developed even further.

A basis for successful prediction is in the following few words:

> *If you fear your future,*
> *you cannot steer your future.*

> *If you hold the present close and future dear,*
> *you will be someone who knows, a future seer.*

Regarding fear of the future, fear is often the result of change or impending change. Change strangely makes the human animal uneasy. If you own a dog or a cat, you know their uneasy response when you rearrange the furniture or alter a significant part of the daily routine. Like us, most of these animals are comfortable with consistency, but Bob Dylan stated, "The times, they are a changing," so one who lives the enchanted life, the ideal life, understands that there are consistencies and there are unknown adventures, there may be things that are stable and there may be things that are in motion. Be it home, work, family, friends or society, some of these things are constants while some of these fluctuate. To see the future, in time you must liberate any significant discomfort you may have with the fluctuations, otherwise, fear will freeze you. It will immobilize the mind.

Remember this: **Action negates fear.**

To get over fear, think of the Navy and the training of their new recruits. If one is to be part of this division of the armed services, of course one must know how to swim. The non-swimmers are immediately put into classes, and believe it or not, some of these young, rugged individuals are terrified of the water. One of the exercises requires a jump into the water from a six-foot high diving board with some expert swimmers standing by the ten-foot deep pool if needed. If you watch this exercise, you will witness real fear, but you will also realize that only six feet of air must be traversed in order to defeat the fear. Some of these recruits have to be "pushed," but once they jump in the water, the fear disappears. Action negates fear. Action cures fear. Action is the remedy for fear. If you fear your future, you cannot steer your future.

To have an intuitive feel for what is to come, a future seer must understand the principle of the pendulum. As we discussed earlier in this book, it is the principle of nature's to and fro, the swing and sway of things such as tides, seasons, barometric pressure, and similarly, interest rates, inflation trends, clothing fashions, architectural styles, music preferences, consumer needs and political ideologies. Knowing the precise pace and knowing the exact extremity of the swing are two difficult but not completely impossible feats; awareness of this principle, keeping it part of your conscious knowledge, working with the pendulum, will eventually allow you to develop a fair amount of intuition as to when and how things will shift and change.

A restaurant owner in Chicago has developed and built more than 65 successful restaurants over the span of his career, only 20 to 25 of which have been open at any one time. He has an innate sense for when one of his establishments should be phased out. He has an equal sense for the location and the timing for the opening of his new restaurant concepts. He does his research, he consults with experts and he combines this knowledge with his intuitive feel for decision making. It is as if he can predict the kind of food, atmosphere, location and marketing which will bring in the customers. As you may know, the restaurant

business is considered a high-risk investment, especially in the highly competitive dining scene of large
cities, but his track record is nearly 100%. He is an
example of someone who effectively combines and
balances his conscious mind with his subconscious
mind. He strides that fine line between the two and
thus he can predict where his next step will take him.

A future seer is also someone who tends to be
proactive rather than reactive.

Proactivity involves foreseeing the potential
problems before they occur. In the case of the restaurant owner, in the 1980s one of his establishments had
a 1950s diner-style theme with prices that seemed to
come right out of the 1950s. In order to turn a profit, to
make up for the lower prices, he required a fast
turnover of customers. He foresaw every type of
problem which could slow down his operation. To
assure this quick changeover of patrons (without
rushing people through their meal) his creativity went
to work.

First, he worked on some of the psychological
aspects of the restaurant. Among them, he researched
the chairs people sat on. Since this kind of place did

not have the expectation of comfort with plush seat-
ing, he found chairs that were fine to sit on for 20
minutes to a half hour, but they would not allow
someone to get too comfortable. Even more important, he realized the quicker the food arrived the
sooner the patrons would finish, so he creatively
streamlined his kitchen procedures like no one had
done before. Additionally, to save even more time,
together with the computer firm who supplied his
cash registers, he revolutionized the method in which
an order was relayed to the kitchen. Rather than
having the wait person walk into the kitchen to shout
out an order, then go to the register to ring it up, he
developed a method in which the wait person rings up
the order on a register which simultaneously sends the
order to the kitchen where it appears on a video
monitor. Time was saved, accuracy was improved,
the wait staff had more time for customers, and they
could attend to more tables. Within a few years, this
method became commonplace in many restaurants
throughout the world.

In short, he foresaw the future consequence
of the present circumstance. So he changed the
present circumstance of how orders were communi-
cated to the kitchen, thus he avoided the consequence

of the existing prototypical procedure found in other restaurants.

A personal example of proactivity occurred a few years ago when I was the producer of a citywide music festival. One of the events involved five consecutive performances within the span of an hour from five different historic architectural sites with live consecutive remote broadcasts from each location, followed by a mixing of simultaneous performances from all of the sites as a grand finale. The logistics to make it all work were mind boggling, yet the hour-long extravaganza was executed without a hitch. It even won several broadcast awards. The feat was accomplished by my team brainstorming and foreseeing every incident that could possibly go wrong, and thus we had safety nets where we needed them. Even at that, we could not control everything; there could be a power outage, a severe storm, maybe even war, strikes or civil tumult; anything is possible, but we knew we proactively did everything conceivable within our control and within the realm of reason to help steer the future for us. Thus we were calm, confident and convinced of the success we would attain with this project. Most important we were equipped and ready for the "curve balls" that came our way during the production.

The key to successful brainstorming is simple, but environments in families and organizations must be conducive for administering this key.

It is based in part on Nobel Prize-winning scientist Linus Pauling's response to a question posed to him during an interview. He was asked, "How do you come up with great ideas?" Pauling responded, "You obtain great ideas by having lots of ideas, and then you must have the power of discernment."

If you study the sketchbooks of Ludwig van Beethoven, you would surmise his response to that question would be similar. Beethoven would write a phrase of music then cross it out, then he would write another phrase of music, cross it out, write another, cross it out, over and over until he found the solution. Sometimes he would pen dozens upon dozens of ideas until he found the answer. His Seventh Symphony is a masterpiece, every moment seeming inevitable, thus it may sound like it was written effort-lessly, but like most of his music, it did not gush out of him in one fell swoop. He achieved his perfection by writing out many ideas until one had a logic and felt right.

Deep inside, most everyone has an abundance of ideas, but most everyone subconsciously judges, critiques and discounts them so that very few or none are consciously realized and verbalized. How often have you seen someone else's creativity and said, "Why didn't I think of that?" You and many others probably did think of it, but deep down it was judged and edited, so much so it never came into conscious being.

Subconscious thoughts and impulses which never come to the fore are often held back because of fear—fear of judgment, fear of failure, fear of ridicule, even fear of work, and even fear of success. The following endeavor will help remove this prohibition.

Exercise #15:

This exercise works well with a team of 4 to 12 people, but it is equally effective for an individual. It may seem trite; at first it may seem ludicrous; but on a regular basis conduct FISH (Fantastic Idea SHower) sessions. Go into a room, put a sign on the outside of the door "GONE FISHING," close the door and IMMEDIATELY start. State a problem which requires a solution. Each participant must begin speaking with the exclamation "I've got it! This is it!" Then the participant must bellow out an idea, and most important, each of the other participants must then IMMEDIATELY exclaim, "That's brilliant!" or "Fantastic idea!" or "That's outstanding!" or whatever comes to mind, as long as the response is blatantly positive and affirmative. One of the people is assigned as a note-taker who records every idea from everyone. Only record each idea; do not attach a participant's name to it.

Don't ponder! Hardly think before you speak. WHEN ONE OVERLY CONTEMPLATES, ONE TENDS TO CONCENTRATE ON THINGS AS THEY ARE, RATHER THAN AS THEY CAN BE. Each participant should barge in whenever they can with the phrase, "I've got it! This is it!," then exclaim whatever solution comes to mind.

During this SHOWER of ideas, every idea is a great idea. Every thought is superb. Every concept is magnificent. And of course, in response, the word "no" is not allowed.

Most likely, people will spew out their thoughts rapidly and continually, but if not, do not be averse to silence. Silence is fine. If there is a lull, let it be so, until someone utters another thought.

The concept here is to create a stream-of-conscious-thought shower, or, if extremely successful, a stream-of-subconscious-idea deluge.

The session should last at least fifteen minutes; thirty to sixty is the norm, but often these sessions successfully go on for hours. Set an allotted amount of time and, when the session is finished, save the notes, leave the room, take the sign down and go on with your other work. Return to the same room the next day with the same team to review the notes. Go through all of the ideas, giving each one complete consideration. Ideas which would have seemed preposterous the previous day, and ideas which never would have been spoken without the positive parameters of this exercise, may now seem exemplary and valuable. With each idea ask, "What if?" Ask, "Why not?" The ideas generated through faithful use of this exercise will astound you.

To execute this exercise as an individual, follow the same procedure remembering that, on the first day, every idea is praiseworthy, so you must verbally laud yourself. In short, always retain Pauling's statement regarding lots of ideas and the ability to discern. Always think of Beethoven and his compositional process. Always bring the thoughts out of your mind BEFORE you edit them.

Speaking of Beethoven, the future seer may wish to intently study art creation. Just as participation in a sport hones teamwork skills and a work ethic which can be applied in other aspects of life, the act of attempting to create a work of art develops the imagination and gives one a comprehension of the process of creativity. You must start with an empty canvas, an empty stack of music paper or a lump of clay to know what it takes to create something from nothing. You may not be good at it, but one should know the universe when it is void, and one should know the universe when you are responsible for filling it. You will gain an insight about nature and a definition of beauty.

To this author, beauty is symmetry with subtle asymmetries. The colors and patterns within the rings of Saturn are finely varied and are not constant throughout. The world is not perfectly round. The face of Marilyn Monroe has a mole on one side. The recapitulation of a Mozart theme is slightly altered from its original statement.

To this author, beauty is also asymmetry with subtle symmetries. The face of the forest when viewed from across the road, the patterns of a single tree with its branches and leaves, the mountains, the waves, the stars (individually and collectively) are all examples of this phenomenon.

Albert Einstein said, "God does not play dice with the universe." My view sees the universe as part order and part chance. It is part law and part random. It is part a dice game, but with rules, with parameters, with guidelines. The universe is not a free-for-all, but then again, it is not a totalitarian state. It may be that it operates with a specific constitution under which its constituents have individual freedoms. The freedoms are what create the difficulty in making specific predictions, but as mentioned, you **can** receive impressions.

The subconscious is aware of organization and freedom; it recognizes both. It is completely familiar and very comfortable with what science calls fractal geometric patterns. It can give definition to the apparent asymmetry and randomness of nature. When you develop a communication with your subconscious, the subconscious can tell you where existing patterns will lead. Thus, you can witness a bit of the future.

If you truly wish to improve upon your ability to foretell, consider this statement:

**Knowledge is power, and
lack of knowledge is power.**

Both knowledge and innocence are bliss.

First we will talk about knowledge: As referenced in chapter four, the future seer is an avid reader. Be a gatherer. Grab information, not just pertaining to your line of work, but to as many topics as possible. Read newspapers. Read magazines. Read journals. Read books. Peruse the web and view some television. We are not talking about having an encyclopedia of facts from A to Z stored in your brain like a *Jeopardy* game show champion. Facts alone will get you nowhere. Rather we are talking about familiarization with what is going on and what has gone on in the world. The more you know about the present and the past, the more you can intuit the future. To be sure, there must be moderation with this gathering of information; you do not want to be in a state where you are too caught up in things as they exist. When you accumulate and assimilate, maintain a state of mind where you question things as they are, where you inquire, "What if?" and "Why not?" Geniuses ask questions, lots of questions. If you wish to see ahead, question the substance of the world as it is so you can imagine it as it can be.

Lack of knowledge is equally important. Often an outsider, someone with little or no knowledge of the existing "parameters" in a particular discipline, creates the solution for which everyone else has been looking. And often these outsiders find solutions no one is looking for; the insiders may have no desire to change since things are going reasonably well, but the outsider frequently has the ability to see further into the future. The use of ceramic material for superconductors is one example. It was an idea which was at first considered preposterous by those who "knew" electricity, yet physicist Dr. Alex Mueller, totally green in the field of superconducting, didn't know any better and won a Nobel Prize for his discovery.

Often it is the young person who just joined an organization or some older person who switches fields who come up with the great ideas. They have not yet been indoctrinated into the way things "should" be. As the new girl or guy on the block, they may also have the extra bit of desire to prove their "stuff" to the rest of the neighborhood. When you are working with someone new, listen to them, ask them their opinions, give them three or four problems which you have not been able to solve. If they come up empty, there is nothing lost; but more than a few times they will come up with some answers. Remember the restaurant owner. There are many reasons why he was successful and this is one of them: He learned early on that the most constructive, creative ideas often came from his new employees.

In order to see the state of the forest, the outsider (or an insider who takes a step outside) is the one who sees the forest from the trees.

Always keep in mind there is no one way to do things. There is no "correct" way. There is no "impossible." There is no "unattainable." If someone comes up to you and says, "We don't do things that way around here," or if someone says, "We tried that before and it didn't work," or if someone says, "It's against our policy to do it that way," or if someone says anything remotely like those phrases, then you know these people may know just a little too much.

Knowledge is power, but knowledge without maintaining a child-like state of wonder can paralyze progress.

This innocent state is the same when you seek an answer from the pendulum. It is a way of allowing your intuition to have an equal footing with your wisdom. Remember, at every point in time, the future is uncertain. But, at every point in time, savoring the current moment with awe, courage, knowledge, innocence and intuition combined can help you see what is coming.

See the future as a present.
Understand but leave the past.
You may have the gift of prescience
when today seems unsurpassed.

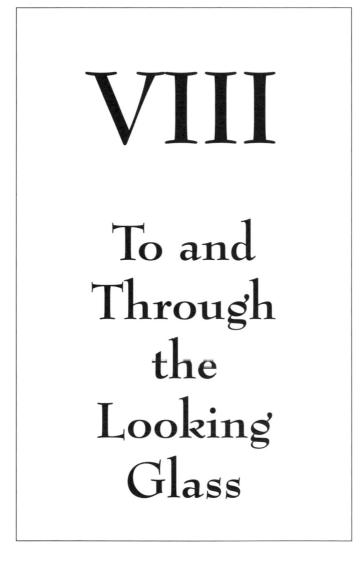

VIII

To and Through the Looking Glass

VIII

To and Through
the Looking Glass

All is within. There are one or two exceptions,
but for the most part, the irony of mankind
is that all which comes to us usually comes
from within us. Someone who is not privy to the
ability of the subconscious will find this statement
hard to fathom.

The whim of luck plays a part in a few things,
but if you are born with reasonable health in a country
of opportunity, that is all the fortune you probably
need. It is all the fate you should expect. Most of your
remaining destiny you can steer on your own.

You may not perceive you have the talents of
others, but history is filled with achievers who had

nothing else but the belief in themselves, the conviction in what they were doing, and the massive ambition and will to do whatever it took no matter what obstacles were present. How else do you explain the mother who lifted the back end of an automobile to release her son trapped beneath? How else do you explain the achievements of Helen Keller? How else do you explain the player you find in just about every sports league who does not have the speed, agility or gifts of other athletes, yet manages to succeed merely through the force of his or her will? How else do you explain the immigrants throughout history who arrive in a new country with no knowledge of the language, no understanding of the culture, and with nothing more than a few clothes in a satchel, who then work their way to success? It happens all the time. In fact, just about every person in the United States is closely related to someone who achieved in this manner.

You may have some of these same qualities of perseverance, but as part of the language we are setting up for communicating with the subconscious, you will now learn something which will give you even greater strength to help your ambitions become a reality. The consequence of this exercise will give you outstanding drive, enthusiasm, dynamism, diligence, focus and confidence. It will also give you the capability to trust and believe in your instincts, aptitudes and abilities.

Exercise #16:

Stand in front of a full-length mirror, or at least a mirror that shows you from the waist up. If you don't have one, get one. Face the mirror straight on and stand erect. Have both feet planted firmly on the floor with your weight equally distributed. Lift your rib cage a couple of inches. Your stomach will flatten. (This rib cage technique is another little secret. Never think of pulling in your stomach. Think of raising your rib cage high. Your stomach will then go in naturally, plus the rest of your carriage will look proud and confident.) Breathe deeply several times until a sense of determination comes over you. Looking in the mirror into your eyes will give you power and strength. Next, think of what you want. Think of a desire. Look directly and deep into your eyes. Now say what you want out loud. Tell yourself you are going to obtain it.

Do this exercise when you wake up in the morning. Do it before an important meeting. Do it before a presentation. Do it prior to seeing someone special. Also, tell yourself there will be nothing standing in your way. Tell yourself out loud that you will be an extraordinary success.

Remember, the subconscious is fully receptive to your verbalizations, especially when you look it in the eye. The subconscious absorbs them like a massive sponge until they permeate through your entire being so you will properly handle important situations without trepidation.

For example, if you are in business and about to meet with an obstinate customer, a feared boss, or someone with whom you need to make an impression, use this technique over and over to help nullify any apprehensions. In addition, practice your presentation in front of the mirror, or most important, practice your initial greeting. Those first 5 to 10 seconds are the key to many successful associations. Visualize those first moments in every detail. Look at your body and the language it projects by how you stand, by how you move your arms, and by the look in your eyes.

Speaking of eyes, if you want powerful eyes, practice this mirror exercise. Within weeks your eyes will develop a strength and an energy that evince your confidence. It is one of the prime benefits of the exercise. To those uninitiated in the ability of the subconscious, this will seem ridiculous; but for those who know, when you feed and nourish your subconscious in this manner, the resulting power emanates through your eyes and by the way you carry yourself. You will have a penetrating gaze that indicates the intensity of your being. Others will recognize it and they will respond positively. All successful body language begins with the eyes.

Regarding body language, there are many good studies and thorough writings on the subject, but effective body language is quite simple and may be reduced to a few key techniques. If followed, you will have a more powerful effect on those with whom you meet and associate.

When you talk with someone, face the person straight on, belly to belly. Do not turn to the side or away even slightly. Even if you are on the opposite side of the desk, face your acquaintance straight on. Your bodies should be parallel. Also, lean ever so slightly forward. Keep your arms open and relaxed. When you are listening, choose one of their eyes; that's right, just one eye, and look directly into it. If it's business, think of how you would like to make this association prosper. If it's romance, think of what the person means to you, or even what it would be like to be intimate. If it's a friendship, think of how much you value his or her importance in your life. In all these situations, have a pleasant, relaxed, friendly, respectful smile on your face. Just as important, while listening, nod gently. Never have a frozen head. Slight, subtle nodding lets someone know you are not only captivated with them, but that you are wholly paying attention. It is also a key in keeping **YOU** focussed on every word they are saying.

If someone looks away, which will happen especially during the first moments of a first encounter, keep these points in mind. In business, keep looking at them, but when they look back, focus on another part of their face, such as the nose or mouth, so your gaze is not as intense. Then gradually look back into their eye.

If you yourself have to look away, never jerk your head. Move your head and eyes away slowly and gracefully. Do the same when you move your head back.

If you are an inherently confident person, effective body language occurs more or less naturally. Most of us, though, need boosts in our confidence level, and strangely enough, even without consciously trying, you may instinctively find yourself using your eyes and body in this effective manner after just a few weeks of employing the mirror exercise. It will happen all on its own.

We mentioned luck a few moments back. The legendary football coach of the University of Alabama Crimson Tide, Bear Bryant, once said, "Luck follows speed." In many sports, the quicker team often receives the good breaks in a game. The same is true for just about everything in existence. He who hesitates may have to wait forever for what he wants.

If you are at a gathering and you see a potential client, a higher level executive from your company, or an influential person with whom you would like to have an association, at the precise moment the opportunity presents itself, go over and make your introduction. Do not wait. Do not ponder it. Seize the moment. Be direct and bold. Coyness and shyness will get you as far as where you are standing now. Again, if you hesitate, you may have to wait even longer, possibly forever.

If you are at a party and you see someone you want to meet because of romantic interest, the procedure may be a little different but it is similar. Most often you should make eye contact first.

For men attempting to establish eye contact with women, understand that women have been brought up to be somewhat demure, so they may look away. But keep looking! If she is interested, she will look back at you within about 45 seconds. This sounds a little absurd, but silently count to 45 in your head and keep looking in an admiring but respectful fashion. If she looks back, perhaps give a nod, smile, then IMMEDIATELY go over to her and begin talking. If you hesitate, the opportunity will vanish. This is not a time for your conscious mind to overly control you. Trust your intuition. Walk over and talk. Say whatever comes out of your mouth. As long as it is not conceited and as long as it is not something negative, whatever you say is fine. Forget about being clever. What you say is just an excuse to start talking with her, and she knows it. Plus, if you have utilized the previous exercise, your words will be spoken with confidence, and that is the most important entity in making an impression.

For women wanting to make contact with men, first understand if you just sit and look coolly away with an expressionless face you will have probably a one in a million chance at the romance you seek. So what do you do? Here is the key. The women who are successful at meeting men make some kind of nonverbal signal of solicitation, and yes, believe it or not, more than a few studies on this subject show women initiate two-thirds of all encounters.

If you are not an initiator, it is probably because you fear you will appear to be too forward. Put your concern aside. Here is the curious irony: Research shows that within a few minutes of the woman's initial overture, the male ego goes to work and the man still feels he made the first move.

Most important, you must do a little more than give a glance at him for a split-second. Even flashing a quick smile before you look away won't do. You may think that's enough, but your chances are still probably one in a million. You must do the following: Look directly at him and **will** his eyes to lock with yours. If you catch his eye, or even if you don't, here are your options.

According to research, the woman who successfully makes the first move makes one of these nonverbal signals: she smiles broadly; or she throws a darting glance; or if at a party or a club, she dances alone to the music; or she flips her hair while looking directly at him; or she keeps a fixed gaze on him; or she looks intently, tosses her head, then looks back; or she "accidently" brushes up against him; or she nods at him; or she points to a chair as if inviting him to sit; or she licks her lips during eye contact; or she walks by him with exaggerated hip movement; or she does anything that shows a bit of an invitation.

Here again, the mirror exercise helps to make you a success with this language of meeting and greeting. Not only will you attain a power, a confidence and a glow, if you employ the mirror exercise, this subtle language will more readily become a reality, and your actions will transpire in a very natural and comfortable way.

For romantic interests between partners of the same sex, much of the same body language often comes into play with one of the parties taking on the more male-type actions while the other party assumes the more female-type role.

No matter who attracts to whom, most important, there seem to be four steps in all of these initial romantic encounters that lead toward a continuation of the engagement, an exchange of phone numbers, or an expressed plan to meet again. Almost all successful romantic partnering begins with a nonverbal signal followed by some simple initial conversation which progresses gradually to a warm turning of the bodies toward each other, leading at some point to an almost imperceptible touch, as in a slight brush of the hand when he hands her a napkin, or a brief, gentle touch of his arm when she speaks. This simple little dance of body language has a great effect on the subconscious of the two parties. If any one of these four steps (a signal, followed by talk, progressing to a body turn, leading to touch) breaks down, there might be a loss of interest, making the partnering more difficult to attain.

If all four take place and flow into each other, two other steps occur. The eyes of both parties soon begin to take an occasional voyage to different parts of each other's head and body. Once this occurs, the most magical of actions follows. The couple begins to move in tandem. They almost mirror each other's movements. What's more, an outside observer would be hard pressed to see who initiated the movement. For instance, they reach for their drinks at the same time, they lean forward simultaneously, their hands may move at the same rate of speed and to the same position. They are practically in total synchronicity.

Of course, following these initial moments of courting, **the long-term success of the relationship depends on a deeper synchronicity, such as the similarity of values and outlook on the world, the ability to truly trust each other, the capacity to unquestionably care, and the skill to genuinely listen and express. Lasting love is mostly the result of two poised, confident people who are as comfortable dancing alone as they are a duet. Each is as comfortable with their own mind and in their own body as they are sharing minds and bodies.**

Whether romance or business, synchronicity is a key to success. In fact, there are many similarities in the actions that lead toward business partnering and the actions that lead toward romantic partnering. Of course the intent is different, but a business person who successfully wins the confidence of a client, employs the art of synchronicity to their advantage.

For instance, upon first meeting a potential customer, a good sales person attempts to match the movements of the customer. If the customer leans on a table, the salesperson casually, naturally and simultaneously adopts the same lean. When the customer straightens and moves away from the table, the salesperson does the action practically at the same time. The synchronicity can also occur over the telephone by matching speech patterns. Whether in person or on the phone, effective initial engagement of the customer involves speaking at the same pace and volume, and with similar formation of speech. If you are based out in a rural area and are calling upon someone in a large city, be prepared for a faster pace of speech. This technique is a conscious synchronicity on the part of the salesperson to affect the subconscious of the buyer. If you believe in the content of your product and truly believe it will help the customer, and if you are an honest individual, then the use of this persuasive synchronicity will help to grab someone's attention, help get them "in tune" with you, help keep their interest, and help affect them to get beyond the fear of making a decision.

In addition to finding, understanding and pointing out the buyer's dissatisfaction over a problem he needs solved, in addition to clearly presenting how your product or service will solve that problem, in addition to establishing your company's credibility, in addition to building urgency into the process, in addition to making the buyer feel he is getting a fair and good transaction, in addition to your passion for the product and for what you do, and in addition to all of these basic elements of the sales process, synchronicity is a valuable tool. It is that extra little something which helps put you over the top. It subtly works because people buy from people who are like them. There is a comfort with familiarity and similarity.

The most fascinating part of this tool is that at some point during the process the customer will begin to move and talk in sync with you, rather than the other way around. The customer will take your lead, now synchronizing with your gestures, matching some of your speech, and coming more into alignment with you. It is a sign that you are communicating effectively with the customer and that they are "moving" toward purchasing your product or service.

This information about meeting and greeting is not intended as a complete guide to sales, to networking, or to romance, but as a description of some important psychological keys. It is a guide about how the subconscious of both parties affects the successful outcome of these encounters. Understanding these principles will greatly enhance your ability to fulfill your desires, and the mirror exercise is the basis for success with these principles. You must literally look in the mirror, pound your fist and tell yourself you are special and you are going to succeed.

Many great orators, public speakers, performers, business leaders, civic leaders, coaches and athletes throughout history have used this same exercise. I have seen people with a ghostly look of fear in their face go into a private room, do the mirror exercise, then come out several minutes later filled with calm and confidence to address a crowd of hundreds. I have seen athletes, exhausted and drained, go into a private room during the intermission of a game, face the mirror, then return to dig even deeper and find energy reserves they never knew they had. And, most significant, I have seen people truly transform their character, their temperament, their aura, their level of self-reliance by executing this exercise over a period of time.

It should be mentioned as a word of caution, the mirror exercise is not about vanity. Vanity has only a modest place here. Yes, it is okay to be a little vain, but only modestly so, and with the understanding that 99% of the mirror exercise is not about looks. It is about believing in yourself and what you have. It is about improving your confidence and magnetism, two qualities which supercede looks, and then manifest naturally in making your outward appearance more effective just by how you move and by the way you use your eyes.

There are people from all over the subjective visual scale of 1 to 10 who succeed in life, whether tall, short, large, small or whatever. The greatest basketball player of all time is bald. His power comes from within and thus his outward appearance shines.

Yes, give attention to the clothes you wear, your hairstyle, your cleanliness, the tone of your muscles, and your overall outward presentation, but moderate your time on this. You (even men) may also wish to see an image consultant. Just like an item on a store shelf, you of course want a great product inside and great packaging outside; when you have both, you have a winning combination, but do not mix vanity with this exercise. Save it for the morning when you shower and get dressed, but even then, keep your vanity in check. The problem with an overly vain existence is that it is part of a perilous wish to be perfect. Ironically, the more perfect we seem to others, the more unavailable for love we appear, and probably the more unavailable for love we are. There is a problem with coming across as too perfect. It can be the antithesis of intimacy. We tend to believe that others will connect with us and admire us if we present a FLAWLESS inner and outer package. Perfect is unapproachable. Perfect is unreal.

Some of the greatest, most acclaimed imperfections are hanging on museum walls. What really makes a person likable and lovable are our vulnerabilities and the confidence to let others see a few of these faults. This is a secret of the mirror exercise. It gives you the self-belief to be true to yourself and true to others about yourself, about all your accomplishments and your imperfections. Even the expert sales or marketing person will let the customer know the drawbacks of the product. It is a key to building trust! Apply the mirror. It will give you the power of sure and secure honesty. Honesty always prevails in the long run. And keep in mind, no matter where you are on that SUBJECTIVE scale of 1 to 10, the way you appear to others will OBJECTIVELY improve through the application of this extraordinary and valuable exercise.

IX

Specialties

IX

Specialties

Here are advanced techniques along with some additional ideas on the impact and influence of the subconscious. They will be extremely useful.

One of the more valuable and functional techniques is the following aid. There are police, fire fighters, military generals, warriors throughout history, explorers and many others who have employed the mechanism you are about to learn. It is a prime example of mind power and the ability to consciously project a thought that others subconsciously pick up.

Exercise #17:

If and when you are in a potentially dangerous, threatening situation, do the following: Imagine a ring of silver suspended around your body in a diameter of about 8 to 10 feet. Literally, you must visualize a silvery, shiny hoop around your being, suspended a few feet from the ground. It is a circle of safety, a ring of protection, impenetrable by danger. Imagine it as a force, a shield.

Of course, do not walk down dark alleys with hundred dollar bills poking out of your pockets; do not walk through a battle zone in an unstable part of the world; do not ask for trouble; but when you find yourself in a potentially volatile situation, utilize this technique. Those who you intuitively feel may hurt you, either physically or even verbally, will tend to be weakened. They may now fear YOU, or at the least, they may ignore you.

The uncanny ability of the mind to project its thoughts is a remarkable faculty. The ability of the mind to intuitively sense danger is equally remarkable. For instance, in a number of rape cases when the events leading up to the incident are recollected, it is often realized that there were several points early on where the victim's intuition said, "Something is wrong here. Something is not quite right," yet she ignored her instincts and her chance to get out of harm's way. If you sense danger, there is no reason to ignore it. NO means NO. It is documented that in not all, but most cases of rape, there are one or more points very early on, prior to the transgression where the woman senses potential peril and can say, "No. I do not need your help with the groceries," or "No thank you, I can walk to the door myself." Of course, in the heat of the moment, while frozen in the presence of danger, such reactions are easier in theory than in execution, but with the mirror and other earlier exercises, you can develop a poise to handle even the most threatening situations. Plus, with the ring of silver exercise, you now have an additional ability to say NO on a subconscious level as well as verbally.

Remember, most animals have intuition. Some are aware of it more than others. For good things and bad things, your intuition talks to you. It is better to know than not to know, it is better to be safe than sorry, so listen. It is part of being that future seer we spoke about in a previous chapter. It will enhance your life and it will protect your life.

Here is a converse exercise to the one above.

Exercise #18:

If you wish to include someone in your life, to bring them closer, to project acceptance, imagine a ring of blue, red or yellow encircling both you and the other person. When in their presence, literally throw a circle of primary color around both of you.

To be clear, you cannot walk down Main Street casting these circles around everyone and expect to befriend the world, but if judiciously employed, if saved for a few select circumstances, this tool will effectively help in making unions and in conveying acceptance and interest.

The thoughts you project mentally about others are usually the thoughts they will return to you. The uncanny ability of the subconscious mind to project its thoughts is a remarkable faculty. On the occasion when you have had a disagreement with someone, or on the occasion when there is tension with someone else, sincerely project good thoughts about the person. Think of their good qualities, the things you like, admire and appreciate. Project these thoughts around them, whether they are present or not. Eventually, you will be pleasantly surprised at the increased ease in resolving differences, in patching things up, in coming to terms, or at the least, if you must part ways, in leaving with some kind of understanding and without bitterness or bad residue.

It is also important to be aware that the thoughts and feelings that emanate from others affect us more than we often realize. Young children will take on the emotional characteristics of their parents, obtaining the same mannerisms, likes, dislikes and fears. Even pets tend to take on the personality of their owners. Whether there is discord or harmony in the household, any new being who is introduced to the home will tend to be susceptible to those emotional qualities.

If you have ever shopped for a new home, even though the owners were not present, you could feel the amount of emotional warmth, care and peace in the home the moment you entered. The atmosphere created by the thoughts of the primary dwellers probably had an impact on your buying decision too. The essence of the people who live in a home or who work in an office is part of the home or office, its walls and its furniture.

Similarly, you may have noticed, if the principal executive of a business is extremely nervous, nearly every person associated with the leader will have a nervous state. Whatever he or she radiates, positive or negative, will have a profound effect on the organization. This applies to managers or any authority within the business. The people at the top set the tone. For instance, if the leader is organized, it is most probable that the employees will take the cue and have orderly desks, offices, procedures and work habits. If the leader is caring, hard-working, creative, knowledgeable, intuitive and a listener, everyone below the leader will most likely acquire many of the same qualities if they don't have them already.

It has been said that we are defined by the people with whom we surround ourselves. Just as one exceedingly negative personality can change the dynamics of a room filled with people, too much interaction with a strongly negative, pessimistic person can reverse your positive polarity. Surround yourself with optimism, confidence and enthusiasm, and your positive demeanor will grow even stronger.

Another example occurs in schools. As you know, many children take on the work habits and personalities of the groups with whom they associate. Place a fairly good student into a lower level math class and the student may soon perform at a lower level. Place the student into a slightly higher level class and the student may live up to the increased expectations. The good teachers and schools are perceptive and continually monitor their students to be certain of accurate placement.

In just about all societies, followers are the majority. Of all the minority groups, the leaders are the minority with the fewest members. The few independent thinkers, the strong, the positive, the self-assured will find a way not to submit to negative group pressure. And once in a while, someone with extreme strength of character may even cause the group to eventually sway to their beat and rhythm.

To repeat from the earlier "Journey" chapter, the moment you decide not to impress anyone but yourself is the moment the road to greatness begins.

Speaking of something that stands out, here follows an impressive exercise, but it may not work right away for everyone. Most important, it must not be attempted until you have mastered the hand-held pendulum procedures detailed earlier in this book. For those who work hard to execute this exercise, it is a remarkable thing to experience and watch.

Exercise #19:

Sit at an empty table. Place an empty, clear, dry, label-less wine bottle a foot or two away from you. With the bottle's cork, push a straight pin or a nail into its bottom. Attach the string end of a pendulum to the pin or nail, then place the cork and the hanging pendulum into the bottle. Place the palms of your hands on the table a foot away from either side of the bottle. Ask a question and watch the pendulum respond.

This is a more advanced, even more extraordinary means of utilizing the pendulum. If you wish to use the pendulum in this manner, do it with the exercises for the hand-held pendulum from earlier in the book, especially EXERCISE #1 where you already know the answers, then progress to #2 and #3, skip #4, and continue with #5 through #8.

In place of the wine bottle, you may also use a clear juice bottle which will allow for a larger size pendulum and a greater swing. Use one of those permanent bonding cements under the lid to attach the nail, pin or even a hook.

As mentioned, the above exercise may not work for you immediately. It took the author eleven months to realize results while others make it work in minutes. If you are the former, you may wish to put it aside and come back to it every few months. Here is an alternate way of obtaining quicker results: if you have a friend who has read this book and applied the information, the two of you can sit at opposite sides with all four palms on the table and ask questions. I have witnessed almost immediate outcomes when the exercise is done in this manner, but the two people must be knowledgeable and comfortable about their subconscious abilities.

Just for experimentation, curiosity and fun, another variation of the free-hanging pendulum exercise is to place three bottles on the table. Put a completely different pendulum in each one to assist in concentration. See if you are able to make just one of the pendulums swing. It can be done.

Now for the pièce de résistance: for those who wish to reap even greater rewards with this subconscious language of success, the following is a most important exercise. It is an extremely advanced pendulum procedure and its success relies on a complete comfort in communicating with your intuition. You are cautioned not to attempt it until you have thoroughly mastered the previous intuitional exercises in this book. If you wish to optimize communication with the subconscious, and if you are seeking even more precise answers to the questions posed to your subconscious, then one of the primary aims of this book will be met in this next approach.

Exercise #20:

Cut 36 one-inch squares of paper or cardboard. On each of the first 26, print a letter of the alphabet. The others should each have a number from zero to 9. On an empty table, lay them down in a broad semicircle. The order should be consecutive.

Hold your pendulum in the center of the semicircle, equidistant from each of the papers. Ask a question.

As always, when learning a new technique, begin by asking the things you know, for example, your name, your address, your phone number. Then move on to things you have forgotten but others may remember. Then after some time, and after receiving reliable answers to these questions, begin making more pertinent, meaningful inquiries.

Take your time with this exercise. The duration for receiving answers is often greater than with the **"YES-NO"** pendulum exercises. You must not be harried by external influences or rushed by your own anxiety. Of course, a quiet, orderly, comfortable setting with a relaxed frame of mind are necessary for accurate results.

Among many possibilities, the above exercise can lead you to one of the ultimate plateaus in subconscious communication. While writing this book, I was asked to make some New Year's Day predictions on national television about events for the coming year. As written in Chapter VII, it is virtually impossible to anticipate how millions of tiny, seemingly negligible, unknown future actions and events will lead to a precise premonition of a few major future actions and events. It is **virtually** impossible, but not **completely** impossible. You can receive impressions, notions of what is to come, and among other techniques, the above exercise was helpful for me in doing so. The words "astro," "emergency" and "rescue" were spelled out using this alphabet-pendulum technique. Another response included the words "new" and "dinosaur." Other messages were more cryptic and they required considerable deciphering and interpreting, but in all I presented nine predictions on this show in what they called **FRIEDMAN'S FORECAST**. At the end of the year, six of the nine predictions came to pass. In the succeeding two years leading up to the publishing of this book, I maintained a better than seventy percent accuracy.

Obviously, years of work developing and understanding a language of communicating with my subconscious made this extraordinary experience of true foresight a reality, and in time the same may be possible for you. Keep in mind, it took three full days for the prognostications to take shape and make sense, so as implied above, the phrase "patience is a virtue" applies perhaps more than ever with this penultimate exercise in order to achieve results.

•

So there you have it. You now have reached a vantage point where you have assimilated twenty-one exercises and numerous ideas on the power of the hidden mind. You will find in time, your intuitive abilities will be heightened and the awareness of your subconscious will be expanded.

This is important: **The astonishing part is that eventually, even without a pendulum, goblet or any device, you will begin to know things and not have any idea why you know them.** You will sense things never before possible for you. In fact, all of your senses will be heightened. You may see what is coming, you may perceive other people's thoughts, you may walk with a little more elevation and determination, and what was previously unattainable for you may now be attainable.

Furthermore, when you make goals for yourself, they may become more like predictions, accurate predictions of the future, aspirations that come true.

A few words of caution: Do not attempt to use the techniques in this book for purposes of gambling. The text is written for men and women who want to succeed in life. The science presented is mostly about human beings, and it is not about the actions of inanimate objects like numbered ping pong balls or dice. Yes, with his or her subconscious, the gambler may, on occasion, set in operation the forces that bring about an occasional manifestation of luck, but there are more sound means of attaining remuneration.

One of the themes of this book is the principle of balance and moderation. If games of chance are something you enjoy as entertainment, play them, but make an honestly affordable, moderate and reasonable limit for yourself, then get out. Whereas life is designed for you to win, these games are designed for you to lose (Why else do casino owners privately refer to slot machines as "mouse traps?"). One reformed gambler I met put it this way: "Put yer money on yer life, 'cause there ain't no winnin' with the games. If ya bet fast ya can't last. If ya bet slow ya gotta go. Now ya know."

X

The
Small
Spherical
Magnet

X

The Small
Spherical Magnet

We have worked on eliminating the guess-work in knowing what your subconscious is telling you. We have worked on a language that feeds the subconscious with your primary desire so your subconscious will help make it materialize. We have worked on a method, a language, a means of communicating with the subconscious so you may receive reliable answers and verify your hunches. We have learned how to heighten your creativity and explore parts of the mind usually unavailable to you. We have explored specific ideas on how you can better view the future, shape your future, and see what lies ahead. We have learned how your subconscious growth can affect the strength in your eyes

159

and body language. We have talked about balancing your logic with your intuition. We have elaborated on the deed of reciprocating the gift of creativity. We have discovered the pendulum metaphor for the swing and sway, the tension and release, of all things in nature.

As mentioned before, a few people do not seem to need the exercises presented in these pages to communicate with the subconscious and achieve success. As cited in a number of examples, there are those who effectively tap their subconscious without any conscious knowledge of this information; their ability is natural, or they were influenced by someone in the early stages of life, or they acquired it from a mentor. There are even those who scoff at this kind of "mind stuff;" they denounce the idea of thought power, yet almost every one of them, if successful, has unconsciously made use of it. Whether believers or not, and whether conscious of it or not, there are many people who possess what is often considered an indefinable "something" that spurs them on to a contented life.

The exercises and ideas in this book are for the great majority of those who want to have that "something." It is for those of us who have no clue how to employ this remarkable power that is within us. This material is for the many of us who try and try but never seem to move forward, and it is also for the naturally advanced people who want even greater attainment. This knowledge is for those of us who want to reach the latter years without regrets, without lament over what we couldn't get done. These exercises are for those of us who need a little more assistance in making magical things happen, so in the end, we feel our century of time was meaningful, fulfilled and enchanted.

As you know, of all the keys presented here, the most important is that satisfaction and success are a matter of application that never ceases. Your entire being, your conscious and your subconscious together, must be involved in the endeavor.

Although the writer cannot claim unabridged all-knowing authority on the topic of the subconscious, there is enough here for you with which to work. The contents took more than a decade to discover, gather and prepare, but there is more to uncover, and you too, along the way, will pull away layers revealing some things never seen before.

Like most everyone, you want peace, you want health, you want some wealth, you want some wisdom, you want adoration, you want an embrace; you wish to experience some of the heaven here on earth.

Believe in your aim, your desire, your wish. It is a matter of cause and effect. You will perceive the outcome. You will conceive the path. You will appreciate the journey. And always keep in mind, creativity is the means to pride and joy, to magic right here and now.

On our planet, the small spherical magnet of great life, there are so many varieties of beings, hundreds of thousands of cohabitating animals and plants, various and sundry breaths—all a remarkable legacy to the experiment called the universe. We may never catalogue or see it all. Some species come and go in unobserved silence, yet for all species and their surroundings, existence is loud. Even the human species exists unobserved by many, but you and each thing are a part of the whole. Your ability to affect the whole is vast. Everything you do, and everything you don't do, affects history.

To be or not to be, that is not the question. You are. You have been. And what you will become is the answer.

What you will become depends on what you will explore. As most of the ocean is unexplored, so too is your subconscious mind. It knows more than you do.

Submerge, breathe easy, and go deep.

Summary of Exercises

Sample Photographs

Photograph #1: A few examples of receptacles for
the goblet gaze (see page 93).

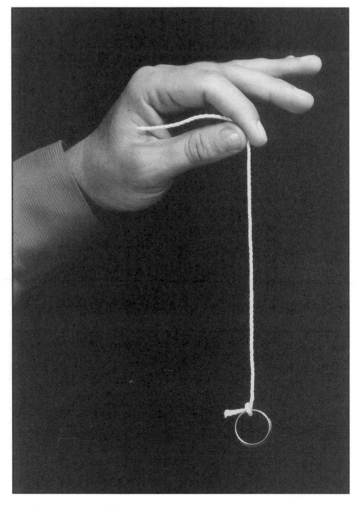

Photograph #2: A "homemade" pendulum in the author's hand, and a proper method of holding the device (see pages 24–26).

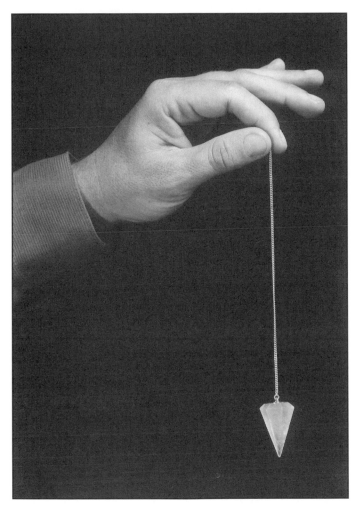

Photograph #3: A pendulum with a chain and a faceted piece of quartz crystal.

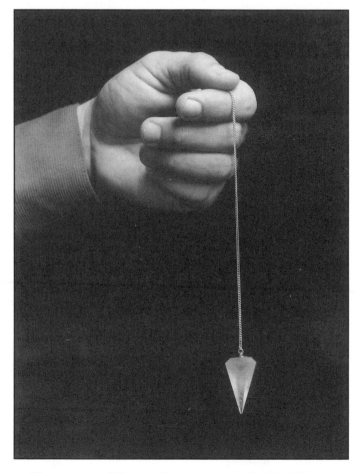

Photograph #4: An alternate method of holding a pendulum device. Although not described in the text, this is equally effective as long as the hand is tilted slightly so the chain (or string or thread) touches only the thumb and forefinger, staying clear of the other fingers.

Notes

On page 20, the definitions of "conscious" and "subconscious" are from *Webster's New World Collegiate Dictionary*, published by Macmillan, 1997.

On page 65, the quote is from the *I Have a Dream* speech by Martin Luther King, Jr. delivered on the steps of the Lincoln Memorial, Washington, D.C., August 28th, 1963.

On page 76, the study on infant massage was conducted by psychologist Tiffany Fields at the Touch Research Institute in Miami, Florida and reported in, among other sources, *LIFE* magazine, the August, 1997 issue.

On page 85, the David Byrne quote is from his song *Once in a Lifetime* from the Talking Heads album titled *STOP MAKING SENSE*, 1980.

Several variants exist (mostly by word of mouth) of the mirror exercise on page 125, but the earliest printed version I can find is in the book *The Magic of Believing* by Claude M. Bristol, published by Pocket Books, 1948. A form of the desire-attainment technique on pages 54 through 60, and a version of the protection technique on page 144 also appear in Bristol's postwar motivational book, though these techniques go back at least to the 19th century.

On pages 131-132, the information on the specific signals women give to men is from the 1985 article "Nonverbal Courtship Patterns in Women: Context and Consequences" by Monica M. Moore from *Ethnology and Sociobiology.*

On page 144, the statement regarding the intuitive sensing of peril well in advance of a rape incident is based on information from the book *The Gift of Fear* by Gavin DeBecker, published by Little, Brown & Co., 1997.

Acknowledgments

Above all, I thank Gerald and Elaine Friedman, my parents, for their unending love, support, and belief in my endeavors.

I give my great gratitude to these friends and associates for their observations and input while completing this book. In alphabetical order they are: Michael Antman, Tracy Arden, Curtis Benton, Roberta Blumenfeld, Edward and Valerie Bovich, Suzanne DeRath, Diane Edelman, Alexandra Friedman, Jeffrey Gitomer, Joe Hislop, Heather McLaren Johnson, Philip Lanier, Mitchell Rogatz, Philip Rosansky, David and Barbara Rosenberg, Nicolae Soare, Jane Terry, Jeffrey Wasson, and Joslyn Zost.

A special thanks to the unique and only Winston the Wonder Dog.

And a debt of thanks to Bruce Bernstein, his insightful red pen, his conceptual mind, and his wife Lynnanne.

Index

175

Photographer: Tom Cruze, *Chicago Sun-Times* (used by permission)

Sidney FRIEDMAN is a seer, composer, phenomenal-
ist, and demonstrator/performer of mind miracles for
individuals and corporations. For the latter, his clients
include companies such as Baxter, Dean Witter, Harris
Bank, McDonald's, Motorola and Quaker Oats. He has
also displayed the power of his mind on numerous
television programs on CBS, NBC, FOX and WGN
television where he is often referred to as "The Haiku
Psychic" for his annual poetic FRIEDMAN'S FORE-
CAST. These predictions have had a consistent accuracy
documented at better than seventy percent. Friedman
was educated at the Eastman School of Music in Roch-
ester, New York, later studied in Sweden on an Ameri-
can-Scandinavian Foundation Grant, and was a
composer fellow at the Boston Symphony Orchestra's
Tanglewood Music Festival. Most recently, he wrote the
music for the PBS television show, *TREASURES OF
THE WORLD,* narrated by Bill Kurtis, and the PBS
television series, *WORLD CLASSICS.*